A–Z

OF

JERSEY

PLACES - PEOPLE - HISTORY

Tracey Radford

AMBERLEY

Acknowledgements

The author and publisher would like to thank the following organisations for permission to use copyright material in this book: the Jersey Heritage Trust, Visit Jersey, the *Jersey Evening Post*. Thanks also to the Very Revd Mike Keirle, the Dean of Jersey and Rector of the Parish Church of St Helier.

Every attempt has been made to seek permission for copyright material used in this book. However, if we have inadvertently used copyright material without permission/acknowledgement we apologise, and we will make the necessary correction at the first opportunity.

Sincere thanks also go to the following people who have given generously of their time and support, whether it be in telling their story, helping source and take images or proofreading: my son Barney De La Cloche, whose work I am proud to feature; my cousin and fellow Jersey Uncovered Blue Badge Tourist Guide Kary Day; Jenny Cabot, Sally Minty-Gravett, Bob Le Sueur, Dacia Diggle, Val Nelson and Neil Mahrer at Jersey Heritage; and Lyndsey Soar at Visit Jersey.

Finally, a loving thank you to my husband Simon for his endless patience, encouragement, and for the hours he has spent taking many of the images in this book and preparing them for print. I couldn't have done this without you.

For my little Jersey girls
Daisy, Kaia and Lani

First published 2019

Amberley Publishing
The Hill, Stroud, Gloucestershire, GL5 4EP
www.amberley-books.com

Copyright © Tracey Radford, 2019

The right of Tracey Radford to be identified as the Author of this work has been asserted in accordance with the Copyrights, Designs and Patents Act 1988.

ISBN 978 1 4456 9390 3 (print)
ISBN 978 1 4456 9391 0 (ebook)

British Library Cataloguing in Publication Data. A catalogue record for this book is available from the British Library.

Origination by Amberley Publishing.
Printed in Great Britain.

Contents

Introduction   4

AA Telephone Box   5
Airport   6

Battle of Flowers   7
Battle of Jersey   8
Boot, Florence (1863–1952)   9
Bouley Bay   10

Claude Cahun (1894–1954)   11
Carteret, Sir George (1610–80)   12
Central Market   13
Clameur de Haro   14
Corbière   14
Crapaud   16

Davis, T. B. (1867–1942),
and Howard Davis Park   17
Dolmen   19
Daniel Dumaresq (1712–1805)   20

Écréhous   21
Elizabeth Castle   23

Flag of Jersey   25

Glyn, Elinor (1864–1943)   27
Gorey   28
Gould, Louisa (1891–1945)   30
Green Street Cemetery   32
Grève de Lecq   33
Grosnez Castle   35

Hamptonne Country Life Museum   36
Havre des Pas   37

Ingouville, George Henry,
VC (1826–69)   39

Jèrriais   41
Jersey Cow   42
Jersey Royal Potatoes   43

Knott, Sir James, and Samarès Manor
(1855–1934)   45

La Caumine à Marie Best   47
La Cotte de St Brelade   48
La Hougue Bie   49

Le Sueur, Bob, MBE   51
Le Sueur, Pierre (1811–53)   52
Les Blanches Banques   53
Lillie Langtry (1853–1929)   54

Minty-Gravett, Sally, MBE   56
Mont Orgueil Castle   57

Noirmont   59
Norreys' Memorial Stone, the Parish
Church of St Helier   60

Old Library   62
Opera House   63
Oysters   64

Parishes   65
Pinacle   65
Public Art   66

Queen Victoria Statue   69

Royal Square, St Helier   71
Rozel   72

St Aubin, Harbour and Village   74
St Brelade's Church and
Fishermen's Chapel   75
St Catherine's Woods   77
St Matthew's Church
(the Glass Church)   78

Towers (Defences)   80

United Club   82

V for Victory   83
Valleys   84
Vardon, Harry (1870–1937)   86

Witches   87

X Marks the Spot for Jersey Treasure:
the Coin Hoard   89

Young, Eric (1911–84)   91

Zoo   93

Bibliography   95
About the Author   96

Introduction

During his mid-nineteenth-century exile to Jersey and Guernsey, Victor Hugo claimed that the Channel Islands were 'fragments of Europe dropped by France and picked up by England'. Indeed, being neither English or French means that Jersey is unusual and unexpected. This self-governing British Crown dependency, 14 miles from the coast of France at its closest point, measures just 9 by 5 miles. However, it makes up for its diminutive size with a huge narrative that goes back to prehistoric times and that continues to develop, ensuring that today Jersey is a vibrant and compelling place to live and visit.

It would be impossible to tell of all the people, places and history that form this island's story, so the author has chosen just a few. While the list of potential subjects is endless, she made the selection based mainly on her experiences as a Blue Badge Tourist Guide and the book looks at what visitors and locals are fascinated by, what they want to see and who they want to hear about, with a few surprises along the way.

Jersey's twenty-first-century culture, natural beauty, agricultural diversity, architectural heritage and fascinating history are unique, and the author hopes that having read the book, you will understand why this island is so special and will want to find out more.

A

AA Telephone Box

In the distant past, when mobile phones were fantasies of science fiction, Jersey drivers whose cars broke down knew that help was never far away ... as long as they belonged to the Automobile Association (the AA). In 1953, several telephone boxes, branded in the distinctive AA livery of black and yellow, were erected around the island to offer members a lifeline if their car broke down. Each member had a key to access the box and could use the telephone inside to contact an AA patrolman who would come to their aid.

As time moved on and technologies developed, more up-to-date AA boxes began to appear, and the 1950s version was phased out from the 1970s. One of the original 1950s boxes still exists in the parish of Trinity thanks to parishioners who campaigned to save it.

The AA Box, Trinity. (© Simon Radford)

Today, while the box is no longer active, it is a wonderful reminder of Jersey's motoring past and also provides locals with a useful landmark when giving or receiving directions. Here is a tip: locals rarely seem to know the numbers of roads used on maps. Rather, directions are generally formed around pubs, landmarks and places associated with friends and family!

Airport

When taking in the golden sands of St Aubin's Bay, it may surprise you to know that for a number of years from 1912, the beach at West Park served as the island's airport. Then in 1937 a new airport was opened in St Peter. This airport benefitted from having buildings and not being dependent on the tides to function.

Four grass runways accommodated flights bringing tourists to the island until 1940 when the German occupation of Jersey began. The commercial purpose of the airport was suspended, and it was earmarked as a Luftwaffe (German air force) base. The Germans set about building concrete runways and hangars for their aircraft, one of which can still be seen today.

The airport resumed passenger services following the island's liberation in 1945 and has served locals and visitors ever since. In the 1990s the airport was expanded, and original structures were incorporated into today's Arrivals Terminal. The distinctive 1930s three leopard badge of Jersey can still be seen above the main door, so when arriving or departing the island, take a few seconds to reflect on this reminder of Jersey's aviation history.

The airport. (© Simon Radford)

B

Battle of Flowers

On the second Thursday of August, Victoria Avenue is closed to traffic as the annual Battle of Flowers takes place along its length. This carnival is a spectacle of floats, dancers, music and colour, and an experience for the whole family.

There is fierce competition for the various awards, particularly between parishes, with the *Prix D'Honneur* the most coveted prize of all.

If you miss Thursday's extravaganza don't worry, you can see it all again the following evening when the floats once again promenade along the Avenue, this time decked with lights for the Moonlight Parade.

The Battle of Flowers has occurred nearly every year since 1902, with just a few interruptions caused by war and occupation. The event began in 1902 to celebrate the coronation of Edward VII and several famous names have been associated with the Battle over the years, including Charlie Chaplin and the racing driver Sterling Moss.

The event's title, the Battle of Flowers, may seem a strange way to describe such a happy occasion. However, it did begin as a battle; once the parade was over spectators

The Battle of Flowers. (© Simon Radford)

and participants would strip the flowers decorating the floats and pelt each other with them. However, over time, as this element of the event became a little too vigorous, the tradition was terminated. Today, while there is no literal battle, enthusiasm for the Battle of Flowers carnival remains as high as it ever was.

Battle of Jersey

Jersey's proximity to France provided Britain with an ideal front-line defensive position against its historic enemy for hundreds of years. This was tested on 6 January 1781 when French forces invaded Jersey.

The Battle of Jersey took place in St Helier's Royal Square between French and British forces of around 600 and over a 1,000 respectively. In under fifteen minutes the outnumbered French surrendered, with each side suffering losses (although the British less so) including both the British Major Peirson and French Baron de Rullecourt.

Today, you can visit key locations of this significant engagement and imagine what it may have been like on that fateful day.

Begin at La Rocque in the east where the French landed before marching into St Helier. Then head to the offshore fortress of Elizabeth Castle that fired its cannons at French troops attempting to attack it from the shore. Walk up Gallows Hill (now Westmount) where the British and Jersey Militia gathered before advancing along what are now Broad Street, King Street and Peirson Place to engage the French in the Royal Square. Here one can see small holes (some covered) on the side of the Peirson pub, said to have been made by musket balls during the battle. In the square, close your eyes and imagine the noise of battle, of men fighting and dying, the smell of gunpowder and the chaos in this small area. Finally, walk across to St Helier Parish Church where Major Peirson and Baron de Rullecourt were buried. While Peirson has a memorial and gravestone within the church, the exact location of de Rullecourt's

Major Francis Peirson by P. J. Ouless.
(Jersey Heritage Collections)

body is unknown, although a simple stone outside the west door ensures that his name is not forgotten, despite him being 'the enemy'.

Boot, Florence (1863–1952)

In a secluded corner overlooking St Brelade's Bay lies the final resting place of one of Jersey's great philanthropists and her husband whose family founded the British high-street chain Boot's the Chemist. Florence Rowe was a Jersey girl whose commercial acumen and vision helped her husband's business flourish and she enhanced the lives of many less fortunate people, particularly women.

Born in St Helier, the young Florence met Nottingham-based Jesse Boot in Jersey when he was convalescing following ill health. They married in 1886 and, perhaps unusually for the time, she played an active part in her husband's expanding business.

Not only was Florence involved in designing stores that maximised the spending potential of shoppers, she also focussed on ensuring that Boot's female employees were properly fed and that their health and well-being was overseen by designated welfare workers.

Concerned that islanders should have access to outside recreational space, Florence gifted and developed land for this purpose and these places, including Beauport Bay and Coronation Park, continue to be enjoyed. With its gardens, play areas and paddling pool, the park remains a favourite place for children and evokes happy memories for older generations, including the author.

The story of Florence would not be complete without mentioning her refurbishment of St Matthew's Church, adjacent to Coronation Park, which is an extraordinary memorial to her husband. However, this is worth an entry of its own so read on.

Florence Boot. (Courtesy of the *Jersey Evening Post*)

Bouley Bay

Down a long winding hill on the north coast, Bouley Bay carves into Jersey's tallest cliffs and is edged by deep water. These features have shaped the bay's story and tales of war, fishing and smuggling abound.

Until the nineteenth century, England's (and therefore Jersey's) relationship with France was volatile and the French attempted to seize the island over the centuries. In 1549 the French landed in the bay and engaged unsuccessfully with the militia on the cliffs above at the Battle of Jardin D'Olivet. This led to the construction of a defensive position overlooking the bay, which became known as Fort Leicester when it was rebuilt in the 1830s. L'Etacquerel Fort was also constructed for extra protection around the same time.

Bouley Bay was not just a place of conflict though; it also featured in the island's nineteenth-century oyster fishing industry when a pier was built to accommodate and protect boats from the elements. In more recent times it has become the location of a Jersey motor-racing institution, the Bouley Bay Hill Climb. This race is for cars, motorbikes and karts, and drivers negotiate the twists and turns of the steep hill with spectators watching the thrilling spectacle from banks above the road.

However, when you venture to Bouley Bay to watch the races, go diving or visit the fortifications, be warned that you may encounter a terrifying creature. It's said that a huge black dog with enormous eyes roams Bouley Bay hunting for people to torment and terrify. A terrible prospect indeed, or did smugglers landing illicit goods on the beach fabricate this tale to keep unwelcome observers away? Who knows, but if you do hear an eerie growl when enjoying the pleasures of Bouley Bay, run!

Bouley Bay. (Courtesy of Visit Jersey)

C

Claude Cahun (1894–1954)

In 1894 Lucy Schwob was born in France and in the early twentieth century this young woman, who became known as a groundbreaking surrealist artist, chose to challenge the conventions of that time.

Reinventing herself as Claude Cahun (Claude is both a male and female name), she and her lover, Marcel Moore (born Suzanne Malherbe), explored the concept of gender-neutrality through photography. In poses and costumes that are neither masculine nor feminine, Claude's images convey her belief that gender identity was a social construct, an issue that resonates in the twenty-first century.

In 1937, the couple relocated to St Brelade's Bay in Jersey and continued their work. However, during the Second World War the island was occupied by Nazi Germany and considering her Jewish heritage, it may be reasonable to assume that Claude avoided activities that could draw attention to herself, but it would be wrong to do so. Claude and Marcel launched a brave but dangerous campaign of resistance against the occupying forces. By writing anti-German propaganda and secreting the texts in

Claude Cahun with Henri Michaux, Grosnez, 1938. (Jersey Heritage Collections)

the pockets and cars of German soldiers, the couple hoped to undermine the morale of Jersey's occupiers.

Claude and Marcel were eventually caught by the Germans and sentenced to death, but fortunately the Allies liberated Jersey before this could happen. Nevertheless, the harsh imprisonment they endured fatally compromised Claude's health and she died in 1954.

Despite being Jewish, the women are buried in the grounds of St Brelade's Parish Church, and they rest peacefully near the sea.

Carteret, Sir George (1610–80)

Standing outside the pub in St Peter that bears his name is a bronze statue of a remarkable individual. Sir George Carteret was a high-ranking naval officer, a statesman and also a privateer who staunchly supported the monarchy during the English Civil War (1642–51) and who led the effort to defend Jersey from Parliamentary forces.

Sir George Carteret.
(© Simon Radford)

Sir George Carteret, who grew up in the parish of St Peter, began his diverse career at just fourteen years old when he joined the Royal Navy. By his early thirties George was a vice-admiral and in 1642 his success as a naval commander prompted the Parliamentarian faction to invite George to head its navy. Always loyal to the monarchy, George refused and instead blatantly supported the Royalist cause by initiating privateering enterprises to 'acquire' as much ammunition and gunpowder from Parliamentary vessels as possible.

In 1643, a beleaguered Charles I agreed George's appointment as Jersey's Lieutenant Governor, tasked with protecting the island from Oliver Cromwell and his Parliamentary forces. This George did faithfully for eight years during which time the king's sons Charles and James were twice given refuge on the island. Following Charles I's execution in January 1649, George ordered the Vicomte to announce the dead king's eldest son as Charles II, even though Parliament now had control of England.

Parliament did eventually subdue Jersey in 1651 despite George's efforts, but in 1660 the monarchy was restored and Charles II showed his gratitude to George for his significant support by elevating him to the positions of Vice-Chamberlain of the Household, member of the Privy Council and Treasurer of the Navy, where he was a contemporary of the diarist Samuel Pepys. He was also granted rights to land in North America now known as New Jersey and where today you can visit the borough of Carteret.

Continuing to serve the king until his death in 1680, George left behind his widow Elizabeth and surviving children. The statue in St Peter remembers a man ever faithful to the English monarchy and of whom Charles II said, 'I can never forget the good services you have done to my father and me [and] you shall find I do remember them.'

Central Market

St Helier's Central Market is a sensory paradise! The smell of fruit, flowers and vegetables, the bustle of stall holders and shoppers, the sight of Jersey's produce and crafts, together with the extraordinary building it all sits within, ensures that this is a place locals and visitors can't resist.

Opened in 1882 as part of the centenary celebrations for the 1781 Battle of Jersey, the market has many notable features. Several sets of original ornate gates provide access and detail some of the items on sale in the market. The exception is the bird that resembles an eagle, which is definitely not for sale at any stall.

Originally the roof was made of glass weighing around 80 tons and supported by thirty-seven cast-iron pillars. However, the pillars now bolster a roof constructed from lighter-weight material. An elaborate fountain draws the eye to the market's centre, while close by Jersey's earliest surviving postbox is a reminder of author Anthony Trollope's improvement of the British Isles' nineteenth-century postal service.

The market is open Monday to Saturday from 7.30 a.m. until 5.30 p.m., apart from Thursday when the market closes at 2.30 p.m.

The Central Market, St Helier. (© Barney De La Cloche)

Clameur de Haro

While Jersey is cosmopolitan and enterprising with, for instance, its restaurants, progressive culture and dynamic finance industry, some quirky practices from bygone times still exist. One such is a little used, but still permissible legal procedure called the Clameur de Haro, which can be enacted by islanders who believe their property is being threatened.

Kneeling, bareheaded and clasping his or her hands, the wronged person recites the following words as near to the site of the supposed crime as possible:

Haro! Haro! Haro! À l'aide, mon Prince, on me fait tort.
(Haro! Haro! Haro! Help me, my prince, I am being wronged.)

The alleged wrongdoer must then cease the activity immediately until it is investigated by the authorities. The wrongdoer may then be fined but if the Clameur is considered to have been improperly invoked, whoever did so will be penalised instead.

The cry of 'Haro!' was possibly intended to be a way of gaining public attention for the imminent pronouncement, while the prince's identity is likely that of Rollo, the tenth-century 1st Duke of Normandy.

This ancient but still valid procedure perfectly highlights Jersey's unique character where old and new harmoniously exist side by side.

Corbière

The south-west corner of Jersey has some of the island's most spectacular views. Here, the wide sweep of St Ouen's Bay is laid out before you and when the weather obliges, the islands of Guernsey, Sark and Herm are visible in the distance. This area is known as La Corbière, which means gathering place of crows, although you are more likely to observe seagulls here these days.

While beautiful, through the centuries Corbière's jagged granite coastline and extreme tidal variations has proved perilous for shipping. One of the most recent maritime crises here was in 1995 when the Channiland Ferry travelling from Sark to Jersey hit the rocks and began to list alarmingly. While there were no fatalities due to the prompt intervention of nearby vessels, a number of the 300 passengers were injured. The disaster is marked by a sculpture of two clasped hands overlooking the place where it happened.

Corbière is dominated by views of an iconic Jersey landmark, Corbière Lighthouse. Built in the 1870s, it was the world's first concrete lighthouse and today, whilst no longer manned, the beam of the automated light reaches up to 18 nautical miles.

Nowadays, this is a great place to enjoy beautiful views. During the occupation, however, the Germans recognised its potential as a place of surveillance and built an observation tower and personnel bunker to monitor threats from sea and air. Since liberation in 1945, the tower has been used by the Jersey Amateur Radio Society and is now a Jersey Heritage holiday let.

Corbière at sunset. (© Barney De La Cloche)

Corbière Lighthouse. (© Barney De La Cloche)

Crapaud

Jersey and Guernsey, the largest Channel Islands, have a long-standing friendly competitiveness and this is enthusiastically expressed at inter-island sporting events such as the annual Murratti football and Siam Cup rugby matches. However, this rivalry extends beyond sport and there is some name calling too.

In meetings between inhabitants of the two islands, any self-respecting Jersey person will dub a Guernsey local with the moniker of 'donkey', allegedly due to their supposedly inherent stubborn streak. In turn, the Guernsey person will address their Jersey counterpart as 'Crapaud', which is a type of toad.

There are several explanations regarding how the toadly nickname evolved and one version is that St Samson was not welcomed by the people of Jersey when he visited in the sixth century and, having received a favourable reception in Guernsey, he showed his displeasure at the slight by directing all the toads and snakes in Guernsey to Jersey. Another explanation is that the name arose because Jersey has the only native population of toads in the British Isles.

Whatever the origin of the name, Jersey people seem to have a fondness for it, so much so that a local magazine of the 1800s was called *The Crapaud*. Two *Crapauds* can also be found nowadays in St Helier. There is *Lé Bouân Crapaud*, a statue featuring this amphibian atop a column inscribed with crimes and appropriate punishments from the 1698 *Code Le Geyt*. This is situated at Charing Cross on the site of Jersey's seventeenth century prison. The other toad lurks amid the Jersey cows in the *La Vaque dé Jèrri* sculpture at West Centre.

Lé Bouân Crapaud. (© Simon Radford)

D

Davis, T. B. (1867–1942), and Howard Davis Park

In 1939, a new park opened in St Helier and its verdant lawns, rose garden and diverse planting from around the globe have delighted those who visit ever since. It provides a space not just for horticultural displays, but also for film festivals and concerts, for children to play and for reflection of the past in its War Graves Cemetery.

Thomas Benjamin Frederick Davis, a Jersey man who made his fortune in South Africa's stevedore industry, was responsible for creating this park in a location linked to a childhood vow. A house called Plaisance once stood on the park's site and as a boy, Davis would collect conkers from its garden. On one occasion the house owner Jurat Falle discovered young Davis and a friend on his land and while he punished both boys, he did so in very different ways. Davis's friend was sent home with a stern letter to his mother, but Davis was locked in the cellar for the duration of the Jurat's lunch. This incensed the boy to such a degree that he there and then promised to one

The Rose Garden, Howard Davis Park. (© Barney De La Cloche)

A floral Jersey flag, Howard Davis Park. (© Barney De La Cloche)

day destroy the house. In time, T. B. Davis the man did just that. Having bought the property from the Jurat's daughter, Davis demolished the house and replaced it with a park that all could enjoy.

Always generous to the island of his birth, Davis's acts of philanthropy increased following his son Howard's death in 1916 during the First World War Somme Campaign and Howard Davis Park is just one example of his generosity. Others include Jersey's first motorised lifeboat, the *Howard D*, and a scholarship for less fortunate boys to Victoria College, a selective fee-paying school in St Helier.

While Davis died in 1942, these manifestations of his benevolence and public spiritedness ensure that the memory of him and his beloved son live on.

Dolmen

Places of religious worship including eleventh-century churches, a Jewish synagogue and Freedom Church, located in a former 1950s cinema, all reflect the diversity of Jersey's spiritual community. They are also tangible manifestations of the island's religious development through time, and structures known as dolmen are evidence of the existence of religious beliefs as far back as the Neolithic period, approximately 6,500 years ago.

Dolmen were created from several upright stones topped by large flat stones, all being of enormous weight. The structure was then covered with tons of earth and stones. The building of these structures or megaliths without the aid of modern tools and technologies would have required a vast workforce and perhaps the very existence of dolmen demonstrates just how motivating and powerful religious belief could be, even in prehistory. Excavations of dolmen have revealed passage graves and uncovered human bones and items such as pottery and flints to accompany those buried there into the afterlife.

There are many dolmen to visit around Jersey. In the east, for instance, are La Pouquelaye de Faldouet and Le Mont Ubé dolmen while in the west visitors can access La Sergenté and Les Monts Grantez dolmen. Whichever of these incredible structures you visit, you will be engaging with those who lived at the end of the Stone Age.

The Faldouet Dolmen. (Courtesy of Visit Jersey)

Daniel Dumaresq (1712–1805)

Eighteenth-century Tsarist Russia may seem an unusual place for a Jersey-born reverend to find himself, but in the 1760s this is where Daniel Dumaresq travelled to at the behest of Empress Catherine the Great.

Born in the parish of Trinity, Dumaresq studied at Oxford University, then began an ecclesiastical career, which in 1746 took him to Russia for the first of several extended sojourns there. He went to St Petersburg as the chaplain of the English Factory, a group of trading agents or factors involved in Anglo-Russian trade, later becoming chaplain to the British Ambassador. Dumaresq mixed in elevated circles at court and his acquaintances included Catherine the Great and her lover. This would have interesting consequences for the Jersey reverend.

Having returned to England in 1762 to be rector of Yeovilton, in 1766 Dumaresq again travelled to Russia, but this time it was the formidable empress who requested his services as an education consultant – an invitation he couldn't refuse. Catherine was an enlightened despot, a monarch who sought to improve society by reforms and developments influenced by the Enlightenment movement in areas such as medicine, religion and, crucially for Dumaresq, in education. Having established systems of primary and secondary education in Russia, Dumaresq continued this role for Stanislaus II of Poland, Catherine's former lover.

Upon leaving Poland, Dumaresq recommenced his ecclesiastical life in the west of England in what must have been a stark contrast to the opulence and glamour of the Russian court. Having refused to accept honours and rewards from Catherine, Stanislaus and even Prime Minister William Pitt, Dumaresq's gift of his many books to Jersey's *Bibliothèque Publique* (public library) suggests that he was both a humble and generous man. Dumaresq never married and died in Bath in 1805.

Daniel Dumaresq, English School Artist, *c.* 1780.
(Jersey Heritage Collections)

E

Écréhous

Six miles off the north-easterly coast of Jersey lies a cluster of islands and rocks known as the Écréhous, and although physically separate from Jersey, they are part of the parish of St Martin. Only three of the islands, Maitre Ile, Marmoutier and Blanche Ile, remain above water at high tide with the little huts and houses that offer temporary accommodation to fishermen and islanders perching precariously above the water line. At low tide, the Écréhous offers a landscape of rocky outcrops, shingle and sandy beaches and seawater pools to explore.

Despite its distance from mainland Jersey, the Écréhous has a fascinating story to tell. It is one of four RAMSAR wetland conservation sites in Jersey, which ensures its natural integrity is maintained. Visitors are likely to spot grey seals, bottle-nose dolphins, terns and little egrets, and see flora and fauna that have developed to survive in this marine environment, and which are not found on Jersey.

However, it's not just wildlife that has inhabited and utilised this reef. Even though it has no fresh water, the Écréhous was once the site of a medieval monastery, and its natural resources have provided granite for building and a local seaweed called vraic, for fertiliser. These remote rocks have also aided those engaged in more shady activities such as smuggling and even kidnapping. In the eighteenth century there was fierce competition between Jersey's rival political parties, nicknamed the 'Charlots' and 'Magots', and neither was above abducting supporters of its opponent at election time and depositing these unfortunate individuals on the Écréhous to prevent them from voting. Thankfully not something that happens in today's elections!

The Écréhous even had its own monarch, a man called Philip Pinel who lived here during the 1800s and who was nicknamed 'King of the Écréhous'.

While smuggling and kidnapping are no longer associated with the Écréhous, it is still a popular place for people to go and the islands are accessed by boat. Several companies offer daytrips to the reef and you can even explore by kayak. It is a magical, unspoilt place and provides a perfect place to escape to, even for just a few hours.

A picnic at the Écréhous. (Courtesy of Visit Jersey)

The Écréhous. (Courtesy of Visit Jersey)

Elizabeth Castle

Situated on a rocky islet and named for Elizabeth I, Elizabeth Castle was once Jersey's principal defensive position. Today the castle's buildings and extensive grounds help visitors discover this small island's vast story.

Construction of the castle began in the 1590s and it was extended over the centuries to meet changing military and defensive needs. Highlights of the castle, of which there are many, include the Tudor fortifications of the Mount with their fabulous views, the eighteenth-century parade ground area and concrete bunkers dating from the Second World War German occupation of Jersey.

However, the story of Elizabeth Castle is not just one of its buildings. It also has a human element with inhabitants ranging from princes and lords to soldiers, their wives and enslaved workers of the occupation. The Governor's House, for instance, was temporary home to historical figures such as Sir Walter Raleigh who was Governor of Jersey from 1600 until 1603, and Princes Charles and James (later Charles II and James II) who sought refuge in Jersey from Oliver Cromwell's forces during the seventeenth-century English Civil War. There is another person who should also be mentioned and that is St Helier, the sixth-century monk who lived on the islet's Hermitage Rock. He suffered a martyr's death and gave his name to Jersey's town.

One of Jersey Heritage's sites, Elizabeth Castle is accessible by foot at low tide and at low and high tide via an amphibious ferry, which is guaranteed to be a fun experience. Cannon and musket demonstrations and guided tours bring the castle to life and visitors leave with an understanding of the important role this island has played in worldwide history.

Elizabeth Castle, St Aubin's Bay. (© Barney De La Cloche)

Elizabeth Castle. (© Simon Radford)

Elizabeth Castle from the keep. (© Simon Radford)

Flag of Jersey

Jersey's flag ,with its white background, red diagonal cross and red shield featuring three gold leopards, is more than Jersey's emblem. It also reflects a critical time in history and can help explain Jersey's relationships with the United Kingdom and France.

The flag's shield and leopards are not only Jersey's official badge; they are also that of the Duchy of Normandy, which Jersey was once part of. However, in 1066, having defeated King Harold of England at the Battle of Hastings, William, Duke of Normandy (William the Conqueror), was crowned William I of England. Jersey therefore became part of this new Norman-English territory until significant events initiated yet another change for the island.

Jersey is not part of the United Kingdom and the flag's Plantagenet crown is a clue to why this is so. Fast forward from 1066 to the early thirteenth century and William I's

The flag of Jersey. (© Simon Radford)

Plantagenet relative John was now on England's throne but had recently lost his Norman lands to the French king. This was a catalyst for events that have shaped the island ever since because, in simple terms, Jersey now had a choice to make. Would islanders remain loyal to the English monarch but face constant threat from an enemy just 14 miles away or would they declare for France? Using tactics of coercion on the one hand and promises of self-government and self-legislation on the other, John persuaded Jersey to ally itself to him, although this was not a unanimous decision.

Thus today, the Bailiwick of Jersey is a self-governing Crown dependency in the British Isles, whose head of state is also the United Kingdom's monarch. This has understandably created some quirky beliefs and unusual customs. A true Jersey local, for instance, may remind you that England is Jersey's oldest possession, while if attending a formal dinner in Jersey, never forget the post-meal Loyal Toast, 'To the Queen/King, our Duke'.

G

Glyn, Elinor (1864–1943)

In twenty-first-century media, stories abound about female celebrities, many of whom are dubbed 'It' girls. The 'It' implies that these individuals are confident, attractive and charismatic. The surprise may be that this term was conceived by a local woman who was not only a novelist but who also made an impact in 1920s Hollywood.

Elinor Sutherland was born in Jersey and her lack of formal education was typical of Victorian girls whose purpose was to marry well and produce heirs. Elinor did get married, to Clayton Glyn, and while she may have not been schooled comprehensively, her childhood interest in reading may explain her literary career as an adult.

Elinor Glyn. (Courtesy of Jersey Heritage, Postcard Collection)

Elinor began writing romantic novels to supplement her income, and these books achieved modest success. However, it was the publication of books considered shocking by the standards of the time, such as *Three Weeks*, a story of seduction and adultery, together with Elinor's affairs with prominent gentlemen, that cemented her fame and notoriety and led to her relocation to Hollywood with its nascent film industry.

Elinor's Hollywood star shone brightly in the early years of the twentieth century. She became a scriptwriter, a director and a respected influencer in this early cinematic age. She is said to have instructed Rudolph Valentino in romantic acting for the screen and it is Elinor who coined the term 'It' in relation to the popular American film star Clara Bow, who starred in the film Elinor wrote, entitled *It*.

Elinor passed away in London in 1943, leaving behind two daughters, her husband having died years before. While not always lucky in love, Elinor was a well-known celebrity who had significant prestige in Hollywood, such a long way away from the place where she was born, No. 1 St Saviour's Road in St Helier.

Gorey

Situated on Jersey's east coast in the shelter of a magnificent thirteenth-century castle, Gorey encapsulates many of the intriguing facets that have made the island what it is and that reflect its story.

When visiting Gorey, you will see fishing boats bobbing in the harbour, shops and restaurants selling local crafts and delicious produce, and you may stroll along the sea wall or up to the castle and look out to the coast of France. Then, if you begin to explore further, you will discover that there is so much more to this charming corner of Jersey.

This poplar location's name has evolved from its twelfth-century moniker of Gorroic to today's more recognisable Gorey, and initially the presence of Mont Orgueil Castle drove development of the area to support the military presence. However, it was in the nineteenth century that Gorey really began to flourish. An oyster fishing industry employing around 1,500 fishermen at its zenith prompted the building of the pier, Le Quai du Havre du Mont Orgueil. Shipbuilding had a major impact too with approximately 150 boats constructed in Gorey's shipyards, and a sculpture resembling the keel of a ship, situated in the gardens adjacent to the pier, lists some of the vessels built between 1820 and 1885.

These businesses together with an emerging tourism industry and arrival of the railway line from St Helier, which ran until the 1920s, shaped the appearance of Gorey forever and looking around the harbour you get a feel for what it would have been like. The harbour and boats, the Victorian hotels still operating as such and the fishermen's cottages (some now restaurants) together create a unique Jersey panorama of history, culture, food and tradition.

Low tide, Gorey Harbour and Mont Orgueil Castle. (© Barney De La Cloche)

Gorey Harbour and the Royal Bay of Grouville from Mont Orgueil. (© Simon Radford)

Gould, Louisa (1891–1945)

Like Bob Le Sueur, whose story also features in this book, St Ouen widow Louisa Gould risked her life to help those in need during the occupation, 1940 to 1945. Eastern European slave workers were brought to Jersey to build the German's numerous defensive structures and were badly treated by their captors. Some islanders bravely decided to help escaped slave workers, and Louisa Gould was one of these because, having lost one of her two sons during the war, she didn't want another mother to go through what she had.

Russian slave worker Feodor Burrij (nicknamed Bill) had escaped and managed to evade the Germans thanks to the help of local man René Le Mottée, who hid Bill until he was informed upon. Luckily Bill was moved on before René was caught and he remained free due to the kindness and courage of Louisa Gould, who sheltered him for nearly two years. From contemporary accounts, including that of Bob Le Sueur, Louisa grew fond of Bill and, owing to her trusting nature, revealed his presence to a number of visitors to her shop. This would be her undoing, and someone denounced her to the Germans.

With prior warning that the German's would search her home, Louisa removed evidence of her illicit house guest and Bill was moved, initially to her sister Ivy Forster's house, and then taken into the care of Bob Le Sueur.

The Lighthouse Memorial. (© Simon Radford)

Regrettably, Louisa overlooked several incriminating items, including a Russian–English dictionary and gift cards addressed to Bill. Having found these, the Germans arrested Louisa, together with her brother Harold Le Druillenec and sister Ivy Forster, who were also implicated in what the Germans considered to be a significant crime.

All three siblings were punished, and although Ivy was given a five-month prison sentence, she served it in Jersey thanks to a doctor falsely stating that she was not fit for deportation. Her sister and brother, however, suffered a worse fate. Louisa and Harold were taken to Germany and incarcerated in two of the Nazi's notorious concentration camps. While Harold did miraculously survive and is believed to be the only British survivor of Belson, Louisa's story was ultimately tragic, and she perished in the gas chambers of Ravensbrück.

Louisa's story was brought to life in the 2017 film *Another Mother's Son*, and she, together with those other islanders who perished as a result of the Holocaust, are remembered on the Lighthouse Memorial in St Helier.

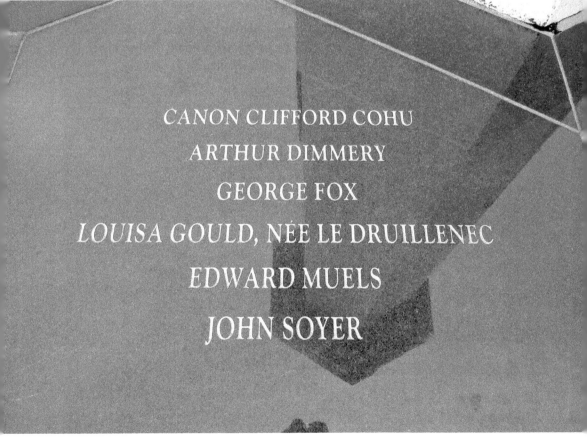

Louisa Gould's name on the Lighthouse Memorial for Jersey's Holocaust victims. (© Simon Radford)

Green Street Cemetery

Green Street Cemetery in St Helier is a site of remembrance and peace, wildflowers and trees. Opened in 1827, the cemetery is a green oasis and its gravestones and memorials are a window into history.

There are several hundred graves, many of which bear traditional Jersey family names such as Gallichan, Le Quesne, La Cloche and Aubin. Unfortunately, some gravestones are so weathered that their inscriptions are indecipherable. However, the text on others remains clear and provides a fascinating narrative on Jersey's past and the many interesting stories there are to be uncovered. Families are buried here, and there are those whose service in Queen Victoria's armed forces reflects Jersey's traditional loyalty to the British crown. There are memorials and gravestones for those who were revered, those who met unfortunate ends and even one gentleman who inspired a political protest from the grave. Let's meet some of them now.

James Hemery, son of a wealthy merchant, was the much-loved Dean of Jersey and Rector of St Helier from 1844 until 1849, and he died from tuberculosis aged just thirty-five. When visiting St Helier's parish church, look above the altar at the magnificent Hemery window depicting the Resurrection, which James' siblings commissioned and dedicated to their parents.

Buried under an elaborate memorial towering over the cemetery is George Le Cronier, Jersey's only Centenier or honorary policeman to die in service. In 1846, while arresting Marie Le Gendre for running a brothel, George was fatally stabbed by

Green Street Cemetery, St Helier. (© Simon Radford)

The Le Sueur family memorial, Green Street Cemetery, St Helier. (© Simon Radford)

the accused. Despite his unfortunate demise, George can, however, claim to be buried under one of Jersey's tallest monuments!

In the mid-nineteenth century, Jersey gave sanctuary to the novelist Victor Hugo and other socialists fleeing from France's turbulent political situation. One such exile by the name of du Taillis died on the island in 1853 but his funeral in the cemetery is remembered more for becoming a socialist demonstration and less for the occasion's gravity.

There are many more names and stories to explore in this Victorian place of rest, reminders of a time of social contrasts, industry and political change.

Grève de Lecq

Grève de Lecq is a popular north coast bay and its sandy beach, pubs and cafés are enjoyed all-year round. Its name perfectly describes its location, with '*Grève*' meaning a 'sandy beach scooped out from the foot of the cliffs' and '*Lecq*' probably originating from the Norse word meaning 'creek', a reference to the stream that acts as a parish boundary between St Mary and St Ouen. Grève de Lecq is more than a seaside paradise; it is also historically significant and retains original buildings and structures that form part of its tale.

Grève de Lecq's stream once powered the watermill that is now the Moulin de Lecq pub. Parts of the mill date back to the twelfth century and while the wheel is no longer used for grinding corn or fulling (cleaning wool), it does give you an idea of how efficient this early manufacturing machinery was.

Tourism in Jersey is not a recent phenomenon and its appeal as a holiday destination developed in the nineteenth century. Victorian appreciation of tranquillity, pure air and sea swimming, together with regular boat services between Jersey and Britain, were crucial in developing this industry. One of Jersey's early hotels, the bay's Prince of Wales Hotel, began welcoming guests at this time and continues to do so in the twenty-first century.

The vulnerability of Jersey's coast to attack led to the construction of many defensive structures at key locations and Grève de Lecq is no exception. The earliest at around 3,000 years old is the Castel de Lecq, a mound or earthworks to the east of the bay. More recent defences include Grève de Lecq Barracks and a round tower dating from eighteenth- and nineteenth-century conflict with France, and also occupation era bunkers and gun emplacements.

So, as you sun yourself on Grève de Lecq's golden sands enjoying a delicious Jersey ice cream, look around, enjoy the view and absorb the essence of times gone by.

Grève de Lecq. (Courtesy of Visit Jersey)

The Moulin de Lecq, Greve de Lecq. (Courtesy of Visit Jersey)

Grosnez Castle

Guarding Jersey's north-west cliffs are the remains of the fourteenth-century Grosnez Castle, intended as a place of refuge for farmers threatened by French attack. It is thought that the name Grosnez is derived from two Norse words '*Grar*' and '*Nes*', meaning 'grey headland', and while much of the castle no longer stands, it is possible to gain a sense of how this granite sanctuary may have looked.

Built in the 1330s around the time the Hundred Years War between England and France was beginning, this location would seem to have made sense as being an ideal place to construct a castle. It perches 60 metres above the sea and the cliffs provide natural defence on three sides with local granite making up the thick landward walls. A ditch, drawbridge and portcullis provided additional security. However, there was a flaw with this castle as there was no natural water supply, which would have impacted on how long people could shelter within its walls.

The castle had mixed fortunes over the centuries. Captured twice by the French during the fourteenth century, the castle was utilised by locals in their defence of Jersey's west during France's occupation of the east from 1461 until 1468. A few years later once the French had been ousted, the Seigneur (Lord) of St Ouen Phillipe de Carteret began to dismantle Grosnez Castle in order to provide building material to fortify his manor house.

In the early 1800s as tensions between Britain and France continued, vital communication with Guernsey was provided by naval signal stations and one is positioned here at Grosnez, which is accessible by a path that dips below the lip of the cliff.

This place isn't just about history though, and visitors can also experience impressive views and glimpse some of the island's feathered residents.

Grosnez
Castle.
(© Simon
Radford)

Hamptonne Country Life Museum

Close to Jersey's coastline are the quiet lanes, fields and farms of the countryside. The island has an enduring agricultural tradition and Hamptonne Country Life Museum transports visitors through this rural history. Once farmed by generations of the same family, it is now owned by the National Trust of Jersey and managed by Jersey Heritage.

The museum reveals much about Jersey's farming background and Hamptonne's special story. Some of the granite buildings date back to the 1400s and several are named after previous inhabitants. These include Langlois House, an upper hall house where a family lived on the top floor, warmed by the heat coming from animals kept below. Hamptonne House was home to Laurens Hamptonne and his family at the time of England's Civil War between Charles I and Royalist supporters and Oliver Cromwell's Parliamentary forces. Despite the distance from England, the conflict impacted on Jersey, which was one of the first places to proclaim Charles II king following the execution of his father Charles I. As he was Vicomte of Jersey, this announcement fell to Laurens Hamptonne.

While some parts of Hamptonne give an insight into the lives of those who lived here, others reveal more about the day-to-day running of a Jersey farm. The labourers'

Hamptonne House, Hamptonne Country Life Museum. (© Simon Radford)

Path to the Syvret House, Hamptonne Country Life Museum. (Courtesy of Visit Jersey)

cottage, for instance, accommodated Breton workers employed during the potato season, while the wash and bake houses were the domain of women who attended to the farm's domestic needs. Part of the Syvret building houses the '*pressoir*' or 'cider barn' where cider continues to be made today. Until the nineteenth century when potato production began to dominate, cider making was a significant industry in Jersey.

Hamptonne's cider-making festival, the Faîs'sie d'Cidre, its farm animals and orchard, together with local craft demonstrations and guided tours, ensure that Hamptonne is truly a living museum, a window into Jersey's country past.

Havre des Pas

According to folklore, footprints discovered on a rock and believed to belong to the Virgin Mary gave Havre des Pas its name ('*empreintes de pas*' meaning 'footprints'). Another explanation is that the area was named for the medieval *Chapelle des Pace* once located here. However the name was derived, this is a popular and attractive seaside spot.

Havre des Pas really began to develop from the early 1800s as families of military men based at nearby Fort Regent were housed here. In addition, Jersey had a profitable shipbuilding industry with Havre des Pas being the site of the Allix shipyard, which operated between 1830 and 1904. A plaque marking the site can be found to the south of Havre des Pas Road.

Victorian enthusiasm for fresh air and sea swimming and commencement of ferry services between England and Jersey helped initiate tourism, an industry that still thrives. Havre des Pas with its sandy beach and proximity to St Helier became a popular resort, and guesthouses and hotels like the Ommaroo today transport you back to late nineteenth- and early twentieth-century holiday times. Well known people who had connections with Havre des Pas include composer Frederick Delius, who stayed at Ceylon House during the 1890s, and T. E. Lawrence (Lawrence of Arabia), who lived in Bramerton House as a child.

The elegance of Victorian design is captured in Havre des Pas's iconic bathing pool, opened in the 1890s. With a pool that captures the sea at high tide and a lido, this has been at the heart of Jersey's swimming culture ever since. The author's grandmother competed in many diving contests here and remembered how important the pool was, not just because of her passion for swimming, but also because it was a place to socialise with her friends during her teenage years.

Havre des Pas is still popular and a place to enjoy and watch the world go by, whether you are strolling along the promenade, sitting at a café or just bobbing around in the sea.

Havre des Pas bathing pool. (© Simon Radford)

Victorian façade of the Ommaroo Hotel, Havre des Pas. (© Simon Radford)

I

Ingouville, George Henry, VC (1826–69)

Since its institution in 1856, the Victoria Cross has been received by several Jersey men. Awarded to those demonstrating extreme courage in the presence of the enemy, one island recipient was George Henry Ingouville.

Born in St Helier, George joined the Merchant Navy in his early twenties and served onboard several merchant vessels. His career in the Royal Navy began in 1851, just before the Crimean War commenced. It was during this conflict, fought between Britain, her allies and their enemy Russia, that George's bravery earned him the accolade.

The conflict mainly focussed on the Crimean Peninsula, although hostilities did take place in other areas and in July 1855 while serving onboard HMS *Arrogant*, George was involved in action against enemy warships at Viborg in the Baltic Sea. During the engagement, George was on the Arrogant's cutter, a small, easy-to-navigate auxiliary boat, when the little boat's magazine exploded. As the damaged cutter floundered under fire, George fearlessly jumped into the sea and manoeuvred the boat away from enemy bombardment, despite being wounded. His heroic actions were recognised and George was awarded the Victoria Cross in 1857.

While undoubtedly couregeous and having won several other medals for gallantry, George's naval career was not without its difficulties as he was imprisoned several times for desertion. He got married in 1861 but little more is known about him apart from that he died in 1869. The cause of his death is uncertain, and it is assumed he was lost at sea. However, the location of his Victoria Cross medal is known and is today held at the Maritime Museum, a fitting reminder of a man who, despite making some unwise decisions during his life, acted with extreme valour and little regard for his personal safety more than once.

George Ingouville's Victoria Cross at the Maritime Museum. (© Simon Radford)

J

Jèrriais

As it is so close to France, you might think that Jersey's traditional language would be French. However, a glance at the island greeting of *bouônjour* and phrase for thank you, *mèrcie bein des fais,* reveals that not all is as you may imagine. *Jèrriais* is the island's historic tongue and while not now spoken widely, the language is as much a reflection of Jersey's past as its castles, churches and dolmen.

Evolving from Norman-French and influenced by ninth- and tenth-century Norse raiders who were active around the Channel Islands and France's Contentin Penninsula, *Jèrriais* developed into a language that is unique to the island. Words still in use today that originate from the Norse language include *hougue* (mound), *mielles* (dune) and *nez* (headland).

The use of *Jèrriais* declined over time as the island's population began to diversify with predominantly French and British residents, and by the nineteenth century it was mainly only country dwellers who continued to speak it. However, during the

Jèrriais signage, the Fish Market, St Helier. (© Barney De La Cloche)

occupation, local will to confound and evade the Germans drove a resurgence of the language, although its use declined once again following liberation in May 1945.

Nevertheless, *Jèrriais* is recognised as a vital part of Jersey's story and the Société Jersiaise, a learned society founded in 1873 to study and preserve the island's history, culture and environment, actively encourages its use. So, as it is still spoken by some islanders these *Jèrriais* phrases may come in handy should a friendly islander strike up conversation with you:

Séyiz les beinv'nu(e)(s) (welcome)
Tch'est qu'est vot' nom? (what is your name?)
Man nom est (my name is...)
À bêtôt (goodbye).

Jersey Cow

No trip to the island is complete without sighting what must surely be the island's most famous resident, the Jersey cow. Not only pretty to look at, these celebrity bovines also have a fascinating history and, most importantly, their milk produces memorable and tasty products, including ice cream and cream.

Evolution of the pedigree Jersey cow really began in the late eighteenth century when farmers were fined if they imported 'alien' cattle onto the island. It developed with the *Jersey Herd Book*, established in 1866, which details all pedigree Jerseys in the island and also those bred around the world, so is a who's who of Jersey cows.

A trio of Jersey cows. (© Barney De La Cloche)

The typical characteristics of this breed have ensured its popularity with dairy farmers globally. Although they are small of stature, Jersey's tolerate a variety of environments and weathers. They are docile, curious and produce creamy milk, which has an unusually high butter-fat content. They are, of course, also charming to look at with their limpid brown eyes and sweet faces.

The habitat of the island's approximately 5,000 cows, 3,000 of which are 'in milk', is naturally the countryside but there is one exception. If wandering through the streets of St Helier, you may come across a herd of these beautiful bovines grazing in the centre of town. This group of bronze Jersey cows or *La Vaque dé Jèrri*, was created by sculpter John McKenna to celebrate the fiftieth anniversary of the World Jersey Cattle Bureau in 2001. The largest member of the group is modelled on a well-known bull who was deservedly called Roselands Extraordinary, and if you peer closely at his neck you may just see engraved his name and sculptor's signature. Extraordinary and his friends are always happy to pose for photos and are a well-known landmark for locals and visitors.

Jersey Royal Potatoes

Jersey's temperate climate provides an ideal environment for growing a variety of crops, the most well-known of which is the Jersey Royal potato. Planted between January and April, these delicious potatoes are harvested from March until July.

Jersey Royals are grown in fields and on coastal slopes or *côtils* and are traditionally fertilised with a local seaweed called *vraic*. The extreme gradient of *côtils* means that planting and harvesting is done by hand, back-breaking work and not for the fainthearted, a task remembered well by St Ouen local, Dacia Le Hegerat. Like most children of farming families, Dacia was expected to help bring in the Jersey Royal harvest. Dacia recalls that when this occurred during term time, an alarming number of farming children suddenly developed a terrible affliction that prevented them from attending school, a condition known as 'potato-itis'!

Like almost everything in Jersey, there's a tale to tell about these tasty tubers, and although potatoes have been grown in Jersey for over 200 years, the unique Royal was a late nineteenth-century phenomenon. It began in 1878 when St Ouen farmer Hugh de la Haye bought two unusually large potatoes with a number of sprouting 'eyes' from a local shop. Having discussed tactics with his farmer friends, Hugh cut the potatoes up, planted the pieces and waited to see what happened. The following spring, Hugh found that the cuttings had produced an early and plentiful crop of kidney-shaped potatoes. Over time, Hugh cultivated these new potatoes and their popularity began to grow, so much so that today the ancestors of those early Royals form Jersey's largest export. Around 30,000 to 40,000 tons are picked annually.

In Jersey, Royals can be bought from many places ranging from supermarkets and the Central Market to farm shops and roadside 'honesty' stalls. In the author's opinion, they are best cooked by gently boiling them and eating with lashings of creamy Jersey butter.

A field of Jersey Royal potatoes (and feathered friends). (© Simon Radford)

Jersey Royal seed potatoes ready for planting. (Courtesy of Visit Jersey)

K

Knott, Sir James, and Samarès Manor (1855–1934)

While not locally born, shipping-line owner Sir James Knott is known in Jersey for his horticultural legacy, located in the parish of St Clement. Samarès Manor's botanic gardens, created by Sir James in the 1920s, are today enjoyed by residents and tourists of all ages.

Born in the north-east of England, Sir James and his first wife, Margaret, moved to Jersey having purchased the manor and its grounds in 1924. Sir James thus acquired the title Seigneur de Samarès (Lord of Samarès). He began refurbishing the house and recognising that Jersey's mild climate was an ideal environment in which to grow a variety of vegetation, he set about establishing a garden featuring shrubs, plants and trees from all over the world. Development of the gardens continued over the years and twenty-first-century visitors can take pleasure from a variety of areas including Discovery and Japanese Gardens, and a play area for children.

Although the gardens are relatively young, the manor has a much longer history. The earliest record of a building here comes from Norman times, but all that remains

The Japanese Garden at Samarès Manor. (© Simon Radford)

of this medieval structure is believed to be an undercroft or cellar. Subsequent inhabitants have remodelled and extended the original manor, with Sir James being no exception. The manor's name derives from the land it was constructed upon, '*samarès*' meaning 'saltmarsh'.

In the grounds is a circular structure that indicates the power wielded by seigneurs in times gone by, and this *colombier* was used to house pigeons that eventually graced the seigneur's dinner table. However, while the seigneur and his guests devoured a succulent bird, pigeons who had so far escaped the cooking pot were tucking into crops grown by the seigneur's poorer tenants. It is not known whether the current seigneur, Vincent Obbard, son of Sir James Knott's second wife Elizabeth, exercises this ancient right!

Samarès Manor herb garden and *colombier*. (© Simon Radford)

Samarès Manor. (© Simon Radford)

L

La Caumine à Marie Best

Overlooking the expanse of St Ouen's Bay is a simple building that, despite its humble design, is known by several names, with each telling a different part of its story.

Built in the late eighteenth century as a powder magazine and guardhouse, the building is one of the oldest military structure in the bay. The remote building then became a place of sanctuary for Marie Best and her children when they sought to escape a smallpox epidemic in 1815 and *La Caumine* is the *Jèrriais* word for cottage.

Once the Best family moved on, the building was left to deteriorate until it was eventually renovated and used as a holiday cottage. It was taken on by Captain John Hilton in the 1930s; then, following Captain Hilton's death in 1975, his widow gifted the cottage to the National Trust for Jersey and the building's next chapter began, this time as Le Don Hilton. The National Trust for Jersey titles such generous donations as '*Le Don*', meaning 'a charitable endowment' and adds the benefactor's name, in this case Hilton.

Rear view of La Caumine à Marie Best. (© Simon Radford)

Front view of La Caumine à Marie Best. (Courtesy of Visit Jersey)

The title that arguably describes this building most aptly nowadays is the White House. Painted a vibrant white, the house is a well-known landmark in the bay, and it can be rented from the National Trust for Jersey. Its location and modest accommodation are perfect for those seeking to get away from it all and who wish to fully experience the coastal beauty of Jersey.

La Cotte de St Brelade

Imagine a landscape of rolling plains populated by woolly mammoth and look in the distance at the mound rising from the flatlands below. This was a familiar sight for Neanderthal hunter-gatherers 250,000 years ago and it is believed they used the elevated land as a place of shelter. Then around 7,000 years ago, melting ice began to surround the mound and sever its attachment to continental Europe at the end of the last Ice Age. Thus, the island of Jersey was formed.

This quarter-of-a-million-years-old story has been pieced together through local archaeology with one of the most well-known archaeological sites, La Cotte de St Brelade, providing thousands of items. Archaeological investigations of this cave ('*La Cotte*' means 'cave') in the cliffs overlooking Ouaisne and St Brelade's Bays began in the late 1800s and early 1900s. Since then, invaluable evidence including Neanderthal teeth, stone tools and animal bones have revealed what type of animals were hunted and how Jersey's earliest inhabitants may have functioned socially. Tools made of flint, the nearest source of which is the island of Alderney around 36 miles away, demonstrate the distances travelled by these Neanderthals and materials from various levels within the cave inform archaeologists about the climate of the time.

La Cotte de St Brelade from below. (© Simon Radford)

La Cotte de St Brelade from St Brelade's Bay. (© Simon Radford)

La Cotte de St Brelade has attracted archaeologists since its discovery, including Prince Charles who attended a dig here with fellow students from Cambridge University in the 1960s. Today, however, you don't need to arm yourself with a trowel and delicately scrape away ancient detritus in order to view these archaeological treasures. Instead, pay a visit to La Hougue Bie and Jersey Museums where you can observe many examples of this invaluable archaeological evidence without getting your hands dirty at all.

La Hougue Bie

Constructed around 6,000 years ago, La Hougue Bie is older than Eygpt's pyramids and believed to be one of the ten oldest man-made structures in the world. *Hougue* means 'mound', which aptly describes the knoll that encloses a passage grave, a place of Neolithic ritual and ceremony and while the exact derivation of *Bie* is unknown, it could be linked to the Hambye's, an old Norman family. Excavated in the 1920s, the mound provides a fascinating insight into the practices of Jersey's early inhabitants.

La Hougue Bie
passage grave interior.
(© Simon Radford)

La Hougue Bie's mound.
(© Simon Radford)

La Hougue Bie is a site where Jersey's ancient and more recent history sit side-by-side. Atop the mound, a medieval chapel evidences the Christianisation of this prehistoric location while nearby, a German bunker is a reminder of the island's twentieth-century occupation. Today, the bunker serves as a memorial to slave workers, forced by the Germans to build their fortifications during this period. In the site museum, items found in archaeological excavations further open the door into prehistory while a replica Neolithic longhouse, constructed by Jersey Heritage volunteers, shows visitors what life may have been like 5,000 years ago.

As well as experiencing the history of this place, at the top of the mound enjoy a stunning panorama of Jersey's lush countryside and, on a clear day, distant views of France.

Le Sueur, Bob, MBE

The occupation of Jersey from 1940 to 1945 was a testing time for islanders and with one German soldier for every three to four residents, violent acts of resistance were few. Nevertheless, expressions of passive resistance were many, particularly following deportation to Germany of non-Jersey-born residents from 1942. One remarkable Jersey man, ninety-eight years old at the time of writing this book, was integral to a dangerous example of this.

Bob Le Sueur remembers the occupation with great clarity, particularly as the timing of the German's arrival scuppered his plans to head to England to join British Forces. Just nineteen when the Germans arrived, Bob's job in insurance enabled him to travel widely on his bicycle and witness aspects of the occupation that would motivate him to defy the Germans.

To Hitler, the Channel Islands were a front-line defence against the Allies. Consequently, the Germans constructed numerous defences, built by those deemed by Nazi racial policy to be '*Untermenschen*' or 'sub-human'. Eastern Europeans including Slavs and Russians were forced into this Nazi project and the appalling conditions in which they barely existed were witnessed by Bob and other islanders. Doing anything to help these poor souls was extremely hazardous for locals, but Bob and a handful of others did take action and set about hiding those forced workers who escaped captivity in their homes and places of work. Bob was responsible for moving many escapees around to avoid detection and managed to conceal Russian forced worker 'Bill' for over a year. Sadly, some brave islanders helping escapees were caught by the Germans and paid the ultimate price including Louisa Gould, whose story is also told in this book.

Today, Bob is determined that his testimony as one of the few remaining who lived through the occupation should be recorded and never forgotten. His strong motivation to 'do the right thing' is apparent and his bravery in helping forced workers was recognised in 2013 when Prince Charles awarded him an MBE (Member of the British Empire) medal.

Bob Le Sueur's portrait by Feodor Burrij.
(Courtesy of Bob Le Sueur)

Le Sueur, Pierre (1811–53)

At the junction of Broad Street, Library Place and Conway Street in St Helier is a monument that honours a man whose tenacity and willingness to take action positively impacted locals in the early years of the Victorian age. Pierre Le Sueur has been described as 'cool and imperturbable, quiet and concise, and in argument almost diabolically clever' and was an advocate who became involved in island politics, a man who made a difference.

During his legal career, Pierre was elected Constable of St Helier, the principal of the parish, and it was in this role that his social conscience came to the fore. At the time, St Helier was overcrowded and living conditions for the poor were unsanitary, with rents often unjustly inflated. Pierre took action and drove initiatives to improve the situation, and in due course landlords who did not adequately maintain their properties were penalised. In the 1840s, a time of hunger for many due to rising bread prices, Pierre effectively prevented disruptive and potentially dangerous bread riots with firmness and fairness and set up a relief fund for those worst affected by lack of nourishment.

Arguably the greatest of Pierre's achievements was the improvement of St Helier's sanitation. Overpopulation in poorer areas, narrow streets and, crucially, sewage running freely in those streets together engendered widespread disease, with several devastating epidemics of dysentery and cholera taking numerous lives in the 1830s and 1840s. Pierre instigated the building of sewers beneath St Helier's streets and improvement of life and health in the town swiftly followed.

The Pierre Le Sueur memorial.
(© Simon Radford)

So successful was Pierre in his endeavours that he was elected as St Helier's constable a further four times. Eventually though, this capacity for hard work seems to have taken its toll and Pierre died in his early forties. The striking granite monument is a manifestation of the esteem in which he was held by his parishioners for all he did on their behalf.

Les Blanches Banques

Jersey has nineteen sites of special interest, areas considered to be of geological, historical, ecological and botanical interest. One is Les Blanche Banques in St Ouen's Bay, noted as one of Europe's most significant sand dune systems.

Les Blanches Banques
and Rocco Tower.
(© Simon Radford)

Les Blanches Banques
and Rocco Tower.
(© Simon Radford)

Les Blanche Banques has numerous plants and wildlife species that are unique to Jersey. The sand dune system supports birds, insects and reptiles like green lizards, grass snakes and skylarks, and plants such as the lizard orchid, dog violet and sand crocus. This delicate ecosystem requires sensitive and considered management to ensure the health of its natural inhabitants and to restrict erosion. Techniques like grazing livestock on the dunes and encouraging the growth of Marram grass, whose roots help stabilise the ever-shifting sands, are routinely employed.

This site is also notable because of the history associated with it. Artefacts and physical remains are evidence that the site was used in the Neolithic age around 6,000 years ago. This archaeology includes flint tools, human bones and *Menhirs* or standing stones, all of which shed light on how these early inhabitants lived and utilised their environment.

During the First World War, the British used Les Blanches Banques as a prisoner of war camp, incarcerating up to 1,500 enemy troops. While little remains of the camp now, some of the buildings' foundations are visible.

Les Blanches Banques is certainly remarkable for those reasons mentioned above, but the area is also important to today's islanders as a place to enjoy recreational and family time. It's an ideal location to walk and the views over St Ouen's Bay are magnificent. Climbing up the dunes and then rolling or running back down has delighted generations of children, including the author, her children and now her grandchildren and even local pooches can join in the fun with an abundance of space in which to run and explore.

Lillie Langtry (1853–1929)

While Jersey girl Elinor Glyn's term 'It' described those she considered charismatic and having sex appeal, it is another local woman who was perhaps the archetypal 'It-girl'. Lillie Langtry was an unusual paradox for this time; both a society lady and actress, this educated woman shocked the upper classes with her extra-marital affairs while attracting admiration for her stunning looks, business acumen and charm.

Emilie Charlotte Le Breton was born at St Saviour's Rectory, only daughter of the Dean of Jersey. Brought up with six brothers, she received an education usually reserved for boys and Lillie grew into a confident young woman.

Following marriage to landowner Edward Langtry and relocation to England, Lillie's beauty and bright personality began to draw attention. Admirers included such literary and artistic luminaries as George Bernard Shaw and Oscar Wilde and well-known Jersey artist Sir John Everett Millais captured her likeness in his painting *A Jersey Lily*.

Despite being married twice, Lillie's liaisons with high-born men, notably Edward, Prince of Wales (later King Edward VII) both intrigued and scandalised Victorian and Edwardian society and this was compounded by her flourishing career as an actress. This occupation led to her touring not just in Britain but also the United States where she was enormously popular, so much so that Texan Judge Roy Bean renamed his town Langtry in her honour.

L

Acting and romance were not Lillie's only diversions. She became a successful racehorse owner and fashion trendsetter, with the Langtry knot becoming a must-have hairdo. She was also mother to a daughter, said to be the result of an affair with Prince Louis of Battenberg.

Lillie died in Monaco but was brought home to rest in St Saviour's Churchyard in Jersey, near her childhood home.

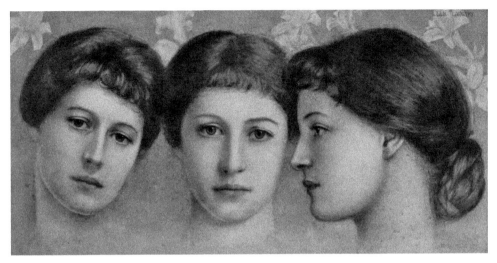

Lillie Langtry by Frank Miles, 1979. (The Jersey Heritage Trust)

Minty-Gravett, Sally, MBE

Living on an island means the sea impacts all residents in one way or another. For Sally Minty-Gravett, the sea is what she calls her 'spiritual home' and her achievements both in and out of the water are extraordinary. Only a special person could swim the English Channel in five out of six decades, with an additional two-way channel swim for good measure, and then swap the bathing cap for ballroom shoes and win a local dancing competition.

Born in 1957 to Anne and Leslie, Sally's passion for swimming started early and she swam before she walked. Before the arrival of public indoor pools in 1969, Jersey's temperate waters provided Sally and her siblings with a maritime playground. By the time she was fourteen, Sally knew she wanted to be involved in swimming for the rest of her life.

Sally's aquatic résumé is remarkable. A successful competitive swimmer, she has achieved multiple English Channel swims over the years and as a qualified swimming teacher, there can't be many island children who haven't been taught by Sally. She is also a Guinness World Record holder, currently being the oldest woman to complete a two-way English Channel swim.

In 2016, Prince Charles presented Sally with a Member of the British Empire medal (MBE) for services to swimming. However, not all Sally's achievements are water

Sally Minty-Gravett MBE. (Courtesy of Visit Jersey)

based. In 2018 she realised a life-long dream and learnt to dance. Having mastered the waltz with professional partner Dragos Patrascu, the couple won a charity dance contest, spinning and swaying to the appropriately watery melody 'Moon River'.

Sally continues to embrace challenge with husband Charlie's support and 2019 objectives include the 12-mile Gibraltar Strait swim, a 'fun' 3 kilometre dip in the Arctic Circle and a 21-mile swim the length of Lake Tahoe in the USA. In 2020, Sally will attempt another Channel swim, a record sixth time in seven decades.

Loving the island in which she lives and possessing a positive can-do attitude, Sally is a great Jersey ambassador. When not submerged, Sally enjoys dancing, food, wine, travel, and most importantly, walking her rescue pup Charlie-Dog.

Mont Orgueil Castle

Mont Orgueil Castle is an imposing medieval stronghold that has guarded the island for over 800 years. Surrounded by cliffs and sea on most sides, the promontory occupied by the castle was recognised as early as the Iron Age as being an ideal site upon which to build a defensive position.

Although built around 1204, the castle's current name was not adopted until the fifteenth century. Mont Orgueil means Mount Pride and once you see the magnificent fortification dominating the east coast skyline, it's easy to understand why this name was given. In fact, when the castle was due to be demolished in the seventeenth century to supply materials for the new and more modern Elizabeth Castle, Sir Walter Raleigh, Jersey's Governor from 1600 until 1603, stated that it would be 'a pity to cast it down'. Thankfully his advice was heeded, and Mont Orgueil has since become one of Jersey's most iconic sights and most visited heritage locations.

Additions have been made to the castle over the centuries to satisfy the requirements of any given time. These include the 1470 Harliston Tower, erected specifically for cannon, and Second World War concrete gun emplacements built by German forces and disguised to look like part of the castle. Altogether the fabric of the castle creates a fabulous architectural and historical timeline, and as you explore the castle's halls,

Mont Orgueil Castle and Gorey Harbour. (© Barney De La Cloche)

towers and ramparts, imagine those who walked here before. There was William Prynne, Puritan critic of Charles I, who was imprisoned at Mont Orgueil, and Prince Charles (later Charles II), who came to Jersey seeking refuge from Oliver Cromwell. Other royal visitors have included Queens Victoria and Elizabeth II.

Run and managed by Jersey Heritage, Mont Orgueil's twists and turns, stories and adventures make this a must-see site on any visit to Jersey.

Above: Stairs to the upper levels of Mont Orgueil Castle. (© Simon Radford)

Left: The Middle Ward, Mont Orgueil Castle. (© Simon Radford)

N

Noirmont

Jersey has its fair share of stunning views and the vista from Noirmont in the south-west is no exception. Not only does it have an impressive panorama, this headland also has great walking paths and is a perfect place to spot birds like wagtails and finches, to enjoy the bright yellow spectacle of gorse and to pick tasty blackberries at the end of summer.

There is a more sober aspect to this imposing promontory and during the Second World War German occupation of Jersey, Noirmont was the location of Batterie Lothringen, a naval coastal battery with commanding views of the island's south, south-east and south-westerly approaches. Much remains of the battery: there are gun emplacements, an artillery range-finder tower and a command bunker which has been scrupulously restored by the Channel Island Occupation Society (CIOS). The command bunker opens to the public on various days throughout the summer months and its various floors are packed with original artefacts and information about this remnant of Hitler's Atlantic Wall defence system. In 1950 the States of Jersey purchased Noirmont as a memorial to islanders who perished during the occupation and a monument on the site tells of this.

A defensive position dating from the early nineteenth century also stands guard here, this one at the foot of Noirmont's steep cliff. The *Tour de Vinde* is a Martello tower

Noirmont Point and the Tour de Vinde. (© Simon Radford)

The Occupation Memorial, Noirmont. (© Simon Radford)

Noirmont country walks. (© Simon Radford)

built in response to the threat of French invasion. The tower today has distinctive black and white markings due to its use as a navigation marker.

Despite its sinister association with past conflict, Noirmont is now a place for all the family to enjoy with its winding footpaths, views and abundant flora and fauna.

Norreys' Memorial Stone, the Parish Church of St Helier

The Parish Church of St Helier, or, as locals call it, the Town Church, is one of Jersey's twelve parish churches and the building paints a picture of Jersey's main town through time. Earliest parts of the church date from the eleventh century and special features include flamboyant window tracery carved from Chausey granite, together with Norman arches and vaulted ceilings. However, as a result of the mid-sixteenth-century Protestant Reformation in which the symbols of Catholicism were stripped from churches, none of the windows, fittings or memorials that predate this episode in history remain.

The church's oldest surviving memorial originates from the 1590s and is situated on the wall of the thirteenth-century Mortuary Chapel, now called St Helier's Chapel. Created from panels of Caen stone, the memorial is to Maximillian Norreys, a relative of the Lieutenant Governor of Jersey Sir Anthony Paulet. This young man fought with the Protestant, or Huguenot, army in France but was fatally injured in 1591. Having been returned to Jersey, his body was buried in the church and the memorial erected.

The text on the stone, much deteriorated over time, is in Latin and the last two lines translate as:

> Him God called away from the midst of the fiery strife of war saying –
> 'My will is that thou shouldst follow not the wars but the stars'

A sentiment perhaps all the more poignant when noting how many memorials there are in the church, which are dedicated to other souls who died fighting for their country.

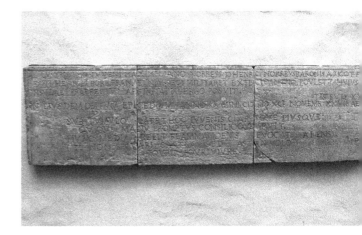

Maximilian Norreys' Memorial Stone, St Helier Parish Church. (© Simon Radford)

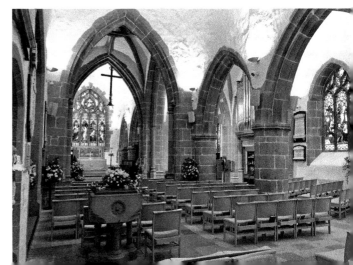

Interior of St Helier Parish Church. (© Simon Radford)

Old Library

Jersey is an island of many forward-thinking 'firsts', such as the establishment of the British Isles' first Chamber of Commerce in the 1760s. The island can also boast of opening the first lending library in the British Isles, a long-held vision of an Oxford-educated Jersey reverend called Phillippe Falle (1656–1742).

Reverend Falle was concerned that both the clergy and those he considered 'the better sort at least of the Laity' should have access to books to expand and develop their knowledge and worldview. Thus, Reverend Falle donated around 2,000 of his own books as well as money to help build a library. Sadly, Reverend Falle died before his dream came to fruition and didn't witness the library's opening in 1743.

Reverend Falle's original books were added to over the years, one benefactor being the founder of the Methodist Movement John Wesley. Visiting the island to preach in 1789, Wesley was impressed enough with the library to gift some of his books to it.

This pioneering library can be found in St Helier's aptly named Library Place. However, don't go there expecting to browse the bookshelves and borrow a volume

The Old Library. (© Simon Radford)

as two other libraries have served the public since. This is why locals refer to Falle's creation as the Old Library. The current library is situated in Halkett Place.

Original features of this eighteenth-century building include Flemish Bond brickwork, dated drainpipes and boot-scrapers by the front door for the 'better sort' of people who once stepped over this institution of learning's threshold.

Opera House

The exterior of St Helier's Opera House is an excellent example of late Victorian architecture with its grand, well-proportioned façade. Opened in 1900, the building was conceived by local architect Adolphus Curry, creator of other notable buildings in St Helier including the Victoria Club (now Banjo's Restaurant) and the Jersey Railway Terminal (today part of Liberty Wharf). The interior design of the theatre is elaborate and elegant with curving balconies that accommodate the dress and upper circles.

The Opera House's story has been marked by varying circumstances. Initially, it was a roaring success following its first performance, *The Degenerates* starring Jersey's own superstar Lillie Langtry; however the rise of talking pictures and cinemas resulted in a decline in business for the theatre. There was a brief resurgence in its popularity during the occupation when some live and film entertainment was permitted. However, following liberation the theatre's fortunes diminished once again.

Thankfully, a combination of private investment, fundraising and government loans during the 1980s and 1990s ensured that the Opera House could be restored to its former glory and today a variety of entertainments keep islanders and visitors entertained

The Opera House. (© Simon Radford)

and enthralled. Among the diverse range of productions available to audiences are musical concerts, ballets, local arts festivals and screenings of live performances from the United Kingdom and elsewhere. There is something for everyone, whatever the interest or age, and the Opera House is a vital element of Jersey's arts scene.

Oysters

Oysters have been eaten by islanders for thousands of years and for much of the nineteenth century, oyster fishing was big business for fishermen from Jersey and further afield. They took full advantage of this plentiful mollusc, but by the 1870s the industry was almost non-existent, mainly due to overfishing.

Happily today, oyster production is thriving again and oysters feature on the menus of restaurants locally, in the United Kingdom and France. The flavour of Jersey oysters is unique and therefore much sought after. Having the third largest tidal range in the world ensures that Jersey's waters provide a clean and nutrient-rich environment for the oysters to thrive in and it imparts a fresh and subtle taste. Local oysters are perfectly accompanied by a glass of crisp, cold Jersey white wine.

Oyster Beds, the Royal Bay of Grouville. (Courtesy of Visit Jersey)

Nine perfect Jersey oysters. (© Simon Radford)

P

Parishes

Throughout this book there are many mentions of the island's parishes, so it seems fair to give them their own account in this text.

Jersey has twelve parishes: St Helier, St Brelade, Grouville, St John, St Lawrence, St Martin, St Mary, St Ouen, St Peter, St Saviour, St Clement and Trinity. St Helier is the most populated parish with around one third of islanders living here, while St Clement is the smallest and St Ouen the largest in surface area. All parishes have some coastline.

The parishes' individual emblems each tell a story. For instance, the two crossed axes of St Helier signify the martyrdom of the monk for whom the parish is named and who is said to have been beheaded by pirates in AD 555. St Peter's symbol of crossed keys are the emblem of this westerly parish and St John's Maltese cross insignia denotes the Knights of St John at Jerusalem.

While Jersey's government has overall authority on the island, each parish has its own municipal structure known as the Parish Assembly. This administers parochial affairs including road management and imposing and collecting rates.

The assembly is made up of parish officers headed by the Connétable, who represents the parish in Jersey's government, and other positions include Procureurs du Bien Public, who supervise parish finances.

At the hub of each parish are a parish church, primary school, parish hall (apart from St Martin, which is a public hall) and, of course, a pub. These are generally located fairly close to each other.

Parishes are an important part of island life that sometimes leads to occasional rivalry between the twelve. This is noticeable during Jersey's annual Battle of Flowers carnival when parishes compete to win awards for the best floats. There are also assertions made by those living in western parishes that west is best – a claim not supported by those from the east!

Pinacle

With its dolmen, *Menhirs* (standing stones) and coin hoard, Jersey is a significant locality for prehistoric archaeology. One of the island's most striking sites is the Pinacle on the north-west coast. This vast granite crag, standing approximately

The Pinacle. (Courtesy of Visit Jersey)

60 metres high, rears up from the sea and is exposed to whatever the weather directs at it. Despite this sometimes inhospitable environment, the prehistoric artefacts and structures discovered here indicate that the Pinacle was an important place for Jersey's earliest inhabitants.

Stone picks and axes found around the Pinacle suggest that weapons were fabricated in this area around 7,000 years ago. Evidence of earthen ramparts point to this strategic position serving as a defensive location later in the Bronze Age, while in contrast, remains of a temple dating from Roman times (*c.* AD 200) have revealed its spiritual use.

Today, whilst the Pinacle's fascinating history secures its place on any archaeologist's 'must-visit' list, the beauty of this rugged spot is not to be missed either. A coastal pathway that passes the rock gives access to breathtaking views of the cliffs, ocean and islands of Guernsey, Sark and Herm (weather permitting of course). At certain times of the year, the ground cover is a vibrant mass of purple heather and, in the sky, Jersey's winged inhabitants and visitors including swallows, oyster catchers and brent geese swoop and soar in the breeze. This is Jersey at its natural best.

Public Art

Jersey has many items of public art like *La Vaque dè Jérri* and statue of George II in the Royal Square, both of which feature in this book. This accessible art reflects the island's enduring custom of commissioning pieces to be enjoyed by all and the tradition has resulted in an abundance of public art, particularly in St Helier. Organisations including the Jersey Public Sculpture Trust and Percentage for Art scheme commission the sculptures, all of which have a story to tell. Here are a few examples.

Deliverance from occupation is celebrated by the Liberation Statue, created by Philip Jackson to mark the fiftieth anniversary of Jersey's liberation on 9 May 1945. Located in Liberation Square, the statue sits on a granite island and features several figures. A British soldier represents Jersey's liberators, a local seafarer is identifiable by his traditional Jersey (sweater) and symbolising islanders who experienced the hardships of occupation are a family group and young couple.

Another piece by Philip Jackson is showcased in the Jardins de la Mer and has a decidedly aquatic theme to complement its proximity to the sea. Two figures can be seen tumbling and diving with two dolphins in *Swimmers II* and the sculpture has fluidity and great energy.

A piece based on Michelangelo's *Madonna Pitti Tondo*, can be found in the north transept of St Helier Parish Church. Created in 2002 by figurative artist John Robinson, this is a stunning contemporary blue glass sculpture depicting the Madonna and Child.

Two Richard Perry sculptures on the Waterfront were commissioned to celebrate important dates for Jersey. The Freedom Tree marks the sixtieth anniversary of liberation. Standing around 6 metres high, this robust oak tree sculpture could be interpreted as reflecting the resilience of islanders during the challenging occupation years. Sensitively complementing the tree is a poem engraved on stone at the base of the tree by local poet Linda Rose Parkes.

Perry's second piece is the Jubilee Needle, created for Queen Elizabeth II's Golden Jubilee in 2002. Cumbrian slate discs secured around a steel core graduate in size to create a smooth cone. This piece of art draws viewers into its variations of colour that change subtly depending on whether the slate is wet or dry.

These are a handful of examples of Jersey's public art and there are many more to engage with. Perhaps take a stroll around St Helier and see how many you can find.

The Freedom Tree. (© Simon Radford)

The Liberation Statue. (© Simon Radford)

The Jubilee Needle.
(© Simon Radford)

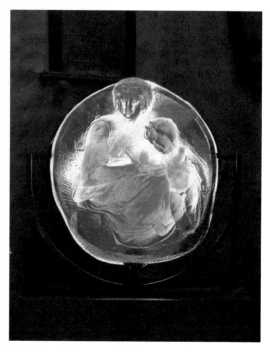

The Blue Madonna, St Helier Parish
Church. (© Simon Radford)

Queen Victoria Statue

Looking towards Elizabeth Castle is a statue of Queen Victoria who, until 2015, held the record as Britain's longest reigning monarch. This bronze statue is adorned with the trappings of state including a crown, orb and sceptre and was devised by sculptor George Wallet to mark Victoria's Golden Jubilee, with the dates of her reign to that point, 1837–87, inscribed on the granite plinth.

The statue is situated in what locals refer to as the Triangle Park next to the Grand Hotel. However, this isn't the statue's original location. Until the 1970s, Victoria stood in a small garden at the centre of the Weighbridge area, today called Weighbridge Place. There she gazed regally upon the hustle and bustle of the harbours, traffic and crowds below. Victoria was relocated to her current position when the Weighbridge area was redeveloped.

Queen Victoria's 1846 trip to Jersey was the first state visit of any reigning British monarch and was accorded the pomp, ceremony and excitement that such a momentous event deserved. It is reported that Victoria was much impressed by the character of her island subjects who gave her a rapturous welcome on both her visits, and that she was quite taken with Jersey's beauty.

Many places in Jersey bear this queen's name, including Victoria Avenue, Victoria College boys' school and Victoria Cottage Homes. These are reminders, not just of Jersey's allegiance to the British crown but also of Victoria's two visits to Jersey in 1846 and 1859.

The Queen Victoria statue. (© Simon Radford)

R

Royal Square, St Helier

St Helier's Royal Square has played a pivotal role in Jersey life for centuries. It has been a marketplace, battlefield and is the political and legal heart of the island, a space for celebration and commemoration. This charming area surrounded by horse chestnut trees is today the perfect place to watch the Jersey world go by.

The square incorporates a vast amount of history, so here are a few highlights starting with the States Chamber and Royal Court building on the south-east side. The Chamber, which opened in 1887, is where the island's government sits. There is public viewing on Tuesdays (and subsequent days if business is not concluded) and visitors can observe the Victorian grandeur of this oak-panelled space and the royal mace, which was gifted to islanders by Charles II as thanks for sheltering him during the English Civil War.

Next to the Chamber is Jersey's highest law court, the Royal Court. Two notable men separated by 800 years are commemorated on its exterior wall with a stone plaque for one and bronze bust for the other. The former is Wace, the twelfth-century Jersey-born author of the poem 'Roman de Brut' that features the story of King Arthur's Round Table. The second is Sir Alexander Coutanche, Jersey's occupation-era bailiff.

At one end of the square are two pubs that have witnessed significant events including the 1781 Battle of Jersey. Appropriately named after the British hero of this engagement Major Francis Peirson, the Peirson pub sits comfortably alongside the Cock & Bottle (formerly the Cosy Corner).

Adjacent to Library Place in a corner of the square is the Picket (or Picquet) House, which until the 1920s served as a base for the military police who managed British soldiers garrisoned in Jersey. Look up to discover George III's monogram on the drain-heads and a sundial designed by local mapmaker and teacher Elias Le Gros.

While exploring the Royal Square, you will be observed by a golden statue of George II, sculpted by John Cheere in 1751. Following its unveiling, the Market Place in which it was placed was immediately upgraded to the illustrious title of Royal Square. Despite being attired as mighty Caesar, you may notice something strange about this seemingly majestic statue. The figure was given two left legs to avoid the cost of making a separate mould for the right leg.

Notwithstanding its regal name, the square is also remembered as Le Vièr Marchi (Old Market), for it was once St Helier's marketplace and today's regular markets

The Royal Square looking west.
(© Simon Radford)

The eastern side of the Royal Square.
(© Simon Radford)

including the Christmas market, La Fête dé Noué, ensure that Jersey's traditions continue in to the twenty-first century.

Rozel

In 1834 Rozel was described as one of 'the very sweetest bays of Jersey' and in the twenty-first century, this little bay has lost none of its charm. A harbour shelters a variety of boats, a sand and shingle beach gently slopes to the sea and picturesque cottages surround the harbour.

Like other bays in Jersey, Rozel's development has primarily been driven by defence, fishing and tourism. As Jersey's closest point to France, appropriate defences were crucial in Rozel, particularly during the Napoleonic War era. One of the military structures was a barracks built in the early 1800s. Strategically positioned overlooking Rozel's beach, the barracks accommodated British soldiers who, despite the persistent danger from France, never saw action here. Today the barracks is a private residence with an outstanding vista.

Jersey's lucrative nineteenth-century oyster fishing industry and a budget of around £2,000 prompted the building of Rozel's harbour in 1829, which provided shelter for the area's oyster fishing boats. Along with fishing, tourism began to impact Rozel at this time and by 1879 visitors were being accommodated in the Rozel Bay Hotel, now the Rozel pub.

Rozel still has a hotel: the Grade II listed Château Le Chaire. The graceful Victorian house was owned by Harriet Fothergill, whose father was respected botanist Samuel Curtis. He recognised the potential of his daughter's Jersey garden for growing the tropical plants that could only be cultivated under glass back in Britain and Samuel's garden became known as the Tropical Gardens of Le Chaire. Guests and locals still enjoy wandering among the abundant vegetation growing in the hotel's grounds and should all the exercise work up an appetite, they can have a bite to eat in one of Rozel's eateries.

Rozel Harbour. (Courtesy of Visit Jersey)

St Aubin, Harbour and Village

The harbour village of St Aubin has bars, cafés and restaurants serving an array of mouth-watering local produce. The area is attractive, an ideal location for that perfect holiday snap, and as you sip your wine or devour your oysters, take a look around and notice the buildings that surround you, all of which tell the story of St Aubin. Here are a few to pique your curiosity.

Affording protection from south-westerly winds, St Aubin has provided a safe haven for shipping over the centuries. From its St Aubin base during the English Civil War, Sir George Carteret's fleet of privateering vessels plundered Cromwell's Parliamentary navy in the name of Charles I. It is possible that part of the Old Court House Restaurant and Hotel on the Bulwarks was used as a court to manage the goods purloined from Parliamentarian ships. If you were a fan of the 1980s television series *Bergerac*, you may recognise the Old Court House as the location of Bergerac's local pub, the Royal Barge.

The construction of St Aubin's pier in the eighteenth and nineteenth centuries was a response to increasing trade coming through the harbour. This included the lucrative cod-fishing industry and the family home of one of Jersey's cod-fishing principals Charles Robin was St Magloire, a house located in St Aubin's High Street, also known as La Rue du Crocquet and the most fashionable place for wealthy merchants to live back then.

St Brelade's Parish Hall in St Aubin is a fine Victorian building, originally a hotel that was also used as a terminus for Jersey's railway. The railway tracks swept round from the seafront having brought trains from St Helier and then continued westwards to St Ouen along what is now known as the Railway Walk, today ideal for walking and cycling.

St Aubin is a favourite spot for locals and visitors and whether you are a foodie, a history enthusiast or just want a stroll, this pretty harbour village has much to discover.

St Aubin's harbour and village. (Courtesy of Visit Jersey)

St Brelade's Church and Fishermen's Chapel

The Parish Church of St Brelade is a building that reflects the island's complex religious history. It is also set in a beautiful seaside location overlooking St Brelade's Bay.

Historians believe this was both a pagan and Christian site before the church was constructed in the eleventh or twelfth century. The oldest parts of the church are the nave and chancel, and over the years the building has been remodelled with additions such as the fifteenth-century south porch and sixteenth-century aisle.

The church has many notable features including its thirteenth-century double *piscina*, unique to the Channel Islands, and locally sourced building materials like limpet shells and beach pebbles. The church's stained-glass windows are exceptional, although comparatively modern. During the Reformation many island churches lost their stained-glass windows to iconoclasm. In the nineteenth century, Jersey glass artist Henry Thomas Bosdet created eight new windows for St Brelade's Church featuring subjects like the Crucifixion and Resurrection.

Next to the church is the Fishermen's Chapel, one of the Channel Islands' few remaining medieval chapels. Evidence suggests that it was built during the eleventh or twelfth century and, like the church, additions and changes have occurred over time. It served as a chantry chapel in the 1400s and arsenal during the Reformation, which perhaps explains why it was spared from destruction at that time. Revealed high on the internal walls are the precious remains of medieval frescoes depicting religious scenes like the Annunciation.

St Brelade's Parish Church. (© Simon Radford)

Interior of the Fishermen's Chapel. (© Barney De La Cloche)

Interior of St Brelade's Parish Church. (© Barney De La Cloche)

There are stunning views of the bay from the churchyard and while walking among the memorials and headstones, bear in mind that a section of these grounds was a burial site for German troops during the occupation. While the bodies were later exhumed in the 1960s and reinterred in a German military cemetery in France, a stone on the wall near the gate adjacent to the slipway remembers the 337 German soldiers who once lay in this sacred and peaceful location.

St Catherine's Woods

St Catherine's Woods is a natural gem in the easterly parish of St Martin. At around 18 hectares (44 acres) and one of Jersey's largest areas of woodland, this is a tranquil green place for those who come to enjoy its paths and streams, flora and fauna.

Within the woods is a reservoir, a favourite spot for fishermen who are often seen waiting for one of the reservoir's carp to take the bait on their lines. Paths take walkers through the trees, with some tracks running alongside a stream that winds around the foliage. Stepping stones cross the stream at certain points, but as the water is not too deep it is often possible, with care and appropriate supervision of children, to wade across the stream. However, Wellington boots are advised if you choose to do this! Children particularly enjoy negotiating the stepping stones and exploring the tangles of trees, paths and vegetation.

The fur and feathered residents of this wonderful space include red squirrels (Jersey's only variety of squirrel), sparrow hawks, warblers and robins, although many more creatures inhabit the area. In the warmer months the ground is a riot of colour from the bluebells, daffodils and foxgloves that carpet the ground and if it rains, the tree canopy should hopefully prevent a serious soaking.

Through the seasons, this woodland consistently charms its visitors with its beauty and family appeal.

St Catherine's Woods. (Courtesy of Visit Jersey)

St Matthew's Church (the Glass Church)

Jersey people have a knack of simplifying the names of places. For instance, the Parish Church of St Helier is usually referred to as the Town Church because, as the name suggests, it's in town! This quirky trait is also applied to St Matthew's Church in St Lawrence, a chapel of ease built in the 1840s.

Known locally as the Glass Church, at first glance it's difficult to understand why as the building is modest in design. However, look at the beautifully decorated glass windows and entrance doors, then enter the church's interior and all is revealed.

This church is decorated with the magnificent creations of innovative glass artist René Lalique. In the 1930s he was commissioned by Jersey's Florence Boot, Lady Trent, to create a memorial to her late husband and the result is a church interior of glass that has been likened to the 'ethereal brilliance of Arctic ice'.

The church contains many exceptional art deco features, including the fluted glass font, the only installation in the church signed by Lalique. At the eastern end a lofty glass cross dominates the alter and four graceful angels watch over the Lady Chapel. The dominant motif throughout, whether on screens, windows or doors, is the *Amaryllis belladonna*, the Jersey lily.

The glasswork in this church is a unique testament not just to Florence Boot's beloved husband Jesse, but also to René Lalique's originality and genius.

Exterior of St Matthew's Church. (Courtesy of Visit Jersey)

The altar, St Matthew's Church. (Courtesy of Visit Jersey)

Towers (Defences)

In the past, Britain's complex relationship with France has often resulted in war and Jersey's proximity to France has therefore provided Britain with a strategic stronghold against its traditional enemy. Thankfully in the twenty-first century, Britain, France and Jersey enjoy a decidedly more harmonious relationship. However, reminders of British-French conflict dating from the late 1700s and early 1800s remain around Jersey's coast in the form of defensive towers.

Situated in areas considered vulnerable to attack and instigated by eighteenth-century Governor of Jersey, General Sir Henry Seymour Conway, the predominant type of defensive structures from this time are called round towers. The towers stand

Starry night at Le Hocq Tower.
(© Barney De La Cloche)

around 11 metres tall with the main entrance on the first floor reached by a movable ladder. The floors had various purposes including gunpowder storage and living quarters for the ten to twelve soldiers manning the tower. The roofs acted as firing platforms for cannon and muskets. Unusual protuberances called *mâchicolations* that project from the top offered protection for the musket-wielding soldiers on the roof as they fired down on the enemy below.

Surviving round towers include those at St Brelade's Bay, Archirondel and Grève de Lecq, with St Ouen's La Rocco Tower the final tower of this design to be built. Other types of defensive tower constructed in Jersey in the early nineteenth century were Martello towers. With a larger footprint and usually consisting of two floors, these towers could accommodate more troops than round towers and Jersey's Martello-style towers include Kempt Tower in St Ouen's Bay and Icho Tower, located off the south-east coast of the island.

These towers are, of course, reminders of turbulent times, but nevertheless, many are now used for peaceful purposes. Some offer holiday accommodation while others make attractive and interesting additions to several island homes.

Rocco Tower. (© Jenny Cabot)

United Club

Jersey's only remaining gentlemen's club, the United Club, is located in St Helier's Royal Square and is an imposing four-storey building with a large balcony overlooking the square. Belonging to a club was often a social, political or commercial necessity for eighteenth-century men who belonged to the ruling upper classes as well as the upwardly mobile middle classes of the nineteenth century. Established in the 1840s, the United Club is an example of such an establishment with traditional facilities including meeting rooms, a restaurant and snooker room.

The building itself has quite an eclectic story and its oldest part is found on the ground floor. In the mid-seventeenth century, this area of St Helier was a desirable place to live and one woman, Suzanne Dumaresq, Dame de la Haule, decided that she wanted to build her house here. Permission was granted on the condition that she construct her house on top of a corn market, which she would also have to build at her own expense. This she did and today the corn market's granite arches can still be seen in the subsequently extended ground floor area, now used as the registrar's office, location of many civil weddings.

This building with its changing appearance and various uses – a market, private home, club and even a hotel – provides an interesting insight into St Helier's social and business development over the centuries.

The United Club.
(© Simon Radford)

V

V for Victory

Although the Royal Square appears in this book, one of its features, a manifestation of one man's courage in the face of adversity, is worthy of an individual entry.

During the Second World War German occupation of Jersey, the occupying force was predisposed to deport 'wrong-doers', and acts of aggressive resistance would have been catastrophic for those committing them, and also for the population in general who may have been subject to German reprisals as a result. However, acts of non-violent resistance did occur and evidence of one such deed is concealed within the granite paving stones of the Royal Square.

Look closely and you will find the letter V (for Victory) disguised among the slabs. It was created in plain sight of the enemy by stonemason Joseph Le Guyader, who was working in the Royal Square, and he covered it with a layer of sand at the end of the working day to prevent it from being noticed. The V miraculously escaped detection and was revealed to all following the island's liberation on 9 May 1945.

When you find the V, notice that the letters E, G and A have been added. These spell the name of the Red Cross ship *Vega*, permitted to come to Jersey towards the end of

V for Victory, the Royal Square. (© Simon Radford)

the occupation and bringing urgently needed food, medical supplies and other items including soap and clothing.

Several more of Joseph's works were concealed around the island including a Star of David-shaped design, incorporated into a granite wall on St Aubin's inner road. All are symbols of defiance and reflect the spirit of Jersey's occupation population.

Valleys

Jersey's coast, cliffs, countryside and town all express aspects of Jersey's distinctive character. Add to that list the island's valleys, many of which have walking paths, an abundance of wildlife and features that offer a window into Jersey's bygone years. There are many to talk about but let's focus on three valleys now, just to whet your appetite.

Mourier Valley on the north coast is a wooded spot that opens out to an expanse of heathland and stretches to the cliff's edge. The stream running through the valley once drove a mill and aqueous features continue with a waterfall that slides off the cliff into the sea below.

The National Trust of Jersey has introduced descendants of animals brought here by Norse raiders over a thousand years ago to manage the heathland. These animals are Manx Loaghtan sheep, distinguishable by the number of horns they have, usually between four and six. Other creatures to observe include choughs, an endangered bird species that has been successfully reintroduced here due largely to successful management of the habitat.

As its name suggests, ferns are very much apparent in Fern Valley, a lush paradise of meadows, woodland, wildlife and flowers. Spot kestrels and buzzards, butterflies and red squirrels as you wander by the valley's steams and under trees that include oak and ash.

It is said that during a visit to Jersey in the mid-nineteenth century, Queen Victoria asked to be taken to one of the island's most beautiful places. She was consequently driven through tranquil St Peter's Valley in her carriage and is reported to have been very impressed. Undoubtedly, this is a lovely place to explore and while the road winding through the valley in the twenty-first century provides a link between north and south, St Peter's Valley is much more than a route from A to B. A unique ecosystem rarely undermined by frost supports an array of plant and wildlife including lichens that thrive in the valley's cool, damp depths. Here you can visit Jersey's only remaining working water mill, Le Moulin de Quétivel, which is powered by the valley's streams and managed by the National Trust of Jersey. If you prefer to experience the area by foot or on a bicycle, there are footpaths winding through the woods and a cycle track that runs the length of the valley, and if that isn't enough, enjoy a refreshing drink at the Vic in the Valley pub, once the Victoria Hotel.

Walking in St Peter's Valley. (Courtesy of Visit Jersey)

Mourier Valley. (Courtesy of Visit Jersey)

Vardon, Harry (1870–1937)

Many Jersey-born people have been successful in the world of sport including Graeme Le Saux (football), Matt Banahan (rugby union) and Serena Guthrie (netball). Perhaps the first local person to achieve sporting superstar status was a boy from Grouville who became a golfing legend.

Harry Vardon recognised his golfing talent early in life, and having turned professional aged just twenty, he went on to achieve great success in the major golfing competitions of the late nineteenth and early twentieth centuries. Seemingly unstoppable, he won the British Open a remarkable six times, as well as the US Open in 1900, extraordinary achievements even by today's standards.

While he died in 1937, his name lives on. He popularized a revolutionary new golfing swing and grip and it is believed that around 90 per cent of golfers use the 'Vardon Grip'. Harry also gave his name to the Vardon Trophy, which is awarded to the golfer with the lowest stroke average by the Professional Golfers' Association of America, and in 1974 he was posthumously inducted into the World Golf Hall of Fame.

A statue of Harry Vardon stands at the entrance of the Royal Jersey Golf Course, situated in the parish of his birth. Sculpted by Gerald Palmer and unveiled by British golfer Tony Jacklin in 2001, the figure is a permanent reminder of a man of whom renowned golfing journalist Bernard Darwin once said 'I do not think anyone who saw him play in his prime will disagree as to this, that a greater genius is inconceivable'.

Harry Vardon's statue at the Royal Golf Course, Grouville. (© Simon Radford)

Witches

The sixteenth and seventeenth centuries saw extraordinary religious change in Europe as the Protestant Reformation challenged the Catholic Church and papal power. It was a time of superstition and those who lived their lives differently to accepted Protestant conventions were therefore perceived as threatening the religion. Such individuals included those alleged to be witches, the majority of whom were women and who consequently suffered from this heightened dread throughout Europe and Jersey was no exception.

In sixteenth- and seventeenth-century Jersey, many who were believed to be witches suffered terrible fates. They were often tortured and those found guilty of witchcraft were executed or flogged. One such unfortunate women was Marie Esnouf and her execution in 1648 was witnessed by many God-fearing islanders. She was burnt but the authorities did show dubious compassion as she was strangled before being committed to the flames. Very different to the fate of 'witches' in Guernsey who were burnt alive.

In the twenty-first century, potential evidence of this historic paranoia about witchcraft may still be visible as you meander through the island's lanes. Look up at the roofs of the oldest houses and you will likely see curious stone ledges jutting out from their chimneys. Superstitious people claimed these were witches' steps or stones, a place for exhausted enchantresses to rest when flying on their broomsticks. The reasoning was that by accommodating the needs of witches in some way, you would avoid their spells and curses. Of course, there is another more rational explanation for these architectural features on Jersey's antique houses. They can be explained as protecting thatched roofs from damp by channelling rainwater away from the straw. A thoroughly reasonable explanation of course...

Witches' steps on the chimney of this traditional Jersey house. (© Simon Radford)

X

X Marks the Spot for Jersey Treasure: the Coin Hoard

There are many tales about the hunt for buried treasure whose location is marked by an X on a map, and fiction became reality for two Jersey men when they discovered a Celtic coin hoard buried in the east of the island. It all began when Reg Mead and Richard Miles heard stories about a local farmer's daughter who had traded ancient coins dug-up in her father's fields for comics. This sparked their thirty-year search to locate where this particular X may be.

Reg and Richard's years of perseverance finally paid off in the summer of 2012 when their metal detectors pinpointed what we now know as the coin hoard. A secret excavation of the hoard by Jersey Heritage and Société Jersiaise archaeologists began, followed by careful and meticulous dismantling of the hoard over several years. This revealed many precious objects hidden within its muddy mass, including over 70,000 coins, gold torques (neck ornaments) and jewellery.

Coin hoard before deconstruction and examination. (Courtesy of Neil Mahrer, Jersey Heritage)

Gold torques from the coin hoard. (Courtesy of Neil Mahrer, Jersey Heritage)

Having discovered the hoard, the next mystery to solve was why it was buried and when. Having scrutinised its contents, Jersey Heritage believes that these valuable items were concealed around 2,000 years ago by Celtic people from northern France who sought to remove their assets from the grasp of the advancing and seemingly invincible Roman army.

The final piece of the puzzle was to gain an idea of the hoard's current worth and in April 2019 the UK Treasure Valuation Committee gave this as a figure somewhere between £500,000 and £2.5 million. However, no matter what its monetary value is, the hoard is an invaluable source of information that can help the people of today better understand those who lived thousands of years before, and items from the coin hoard are displayed at La Hougue Bie (correct at the time of this book's publication).

Y

Young, Eric (1911–84)

Throughout spring, summer and autumn, Jersey's love of flowers is revealed in the island's beautiful private gardens, public-parks and in displays throughout the island. In Trinity there is a floral paradise that is guaranteed to delight those who visit it for around eleven months of the year, whether you are an ardent Orchidist or not. It was the vision of a man with a passion for orchids, that resulted in the creation of a world-renowned orchid foundation.

Born in 1911, Eric Young's fascination with orchids began at an early age and throughout his life he collected and bred a wide variety of these flowers. Successful in business, Eric Young moved to Jersey after the Second World War and in the 1980s began setting up the Eric Young Orchid Foundation.

When visiting the Foundation today, expect a spectacle of colour and beauty as you take in the huge variety of delicate flowers on display. You can also watch the

The Eric Young Orchid Foundation. (© Simon Radford)

Foundation's orchid specialists as they work to nurture the plants and to create new varieties, many of which win sought after accolades at prestigious horticultural events, notably the Chelsea Flower Show.

Sadly, Eric Young didn't live long enough to see his dream fulfilled, however, the Foundation is a glorious floral tribute to this life-long lover of orchids.

Greenhouse at the Eric Young Orchid Foundation. (© Simon Radford)

Z

Zoo

In 1959, one man's quest to save as many the world's endangered species from extinction as possible, led to the creation of a unique zoo in the depths of Trinity. Whilst the word 'zoo' can have negative connotations, Jersey's zoo is a renowned centre of conservation excellence and animal breeding. It is also a beautiful space in which visitors can engage with the zoo's residents, who all enjoy superb care in appropriate natural environments.

The vision of conservationist and naturalist Gerald Durrell, author of the much-loved autobiographical novel *My family and other animals*, the zoo is located in the grounds of Les Augrès Manor, now headquarters of the Durrell Wildlife Conservation Trust. Covering around 32 acres, the zoo is home to a multitude of endangered species, fourteen of which have been safeguarded from extinction by the work carried out here. Success stories include the Mauritian Pink Pigeon, a bird whose numbers dropped to just sixteen in the wild. Thanks to Jersey Zoo, Pink Pigeons raised through its breeding-programme have been successfully released, taking the wild population to over four hundred.

The zoo's *Durrell Conservation Academy* has a vital role to play in the preservation of the world's most vulnerable species. Here, students from all over the world learn about the protection and preservation of endangered species which is vital to enable the zoo's crucial work to continue. Also important is local and global sponsorship through donations, memberships and animal adoption schemes, as well as the support of high-profile individuals, notably the zoo's patron, Her Royal Highness the Princess Royal and Hollywood actor and Jersey-man Henry Cavill, who is a Durrell Ambassador.

When visiting the zoo, expect to see a variety of endangered mammals, amphibians, insects and reptiles, including gorillas and lemurs, boas and tortoises, frogs and cranes. Each has its own unique character and this together with the dedicated staff and stunning setting means that time spent at Jersey Zoo will be remembered for a very long time.

Gorilla enclosure at the zoo. (Courtesy of Visit Jersey)

Gorillas in our midst at the zoo. (Courtesy of Visit Jersey)

Orangutan fun at the zoo. (Courtesy of Visit Jersey)

Bibliography

The following have been invaluable resources:

Balleine, G.R., *All for the King, The Life Story of Sir George Carteret* (Jersey: La Société Jersiaise, 1976)

Corbet, Francis L. M., *The Monuments and Windows of The Parish Church of Saint Helier* (Jersey: The Rector and Wardens, The Parish Church of Saint Helier, Jersey, 2004)

Jersey Heritage Trust (Various), *What's Your Street's Story?* (Jersey: Jersey Heritage Trust, 2014)

Jersey Heritage Trust (Various), *What's Your Street's Story?*: Part Two (Jersey: Jersey Heritage Trust, 2016)

McCormack, John, *Channel Island Churches* (Chichester: Phillimore & Co. Ltd, 1986)

Platt, Colin, *A Concise History of Jersey: A new perspective* (Jersey: Société Jersiaise, 2009)

Syvret, Marguerite and Stevens, Joan, *Balleine's History of Jersey* (Jersey: Société Jersiaise, 1998, 2011)

www.britannica.com
www.cios.org.je
www.jerseybiodiversitycentre.org.je
www.jerseyeveningpost.com/news/2019/04/08/coin-hoard-could-be-worth-up-to-25m/
www.jerseyheritage.org
www.worldgolfhalloffame.org

About the Author

A dedicated historian with a degree in history, Tracey Radford moved to the island, home of her parents and grandparents, in her late teens. Raised on tales of Jersey life from her Jersey-French grandmothers, Tracey's love of Jersey, appreciation of its natural beauty and understanding of its culture and history led to her becoming a site guide for Jersey Heritage, a qualified Blue Badge tourist guide and a founding member of Jersey Uncovered, a team of professional, registered tourist guides whose tours and bespoke experiences help visitors as well as locals discover all things Jersey, from the Palaeolithic era to the present day.

The author, Tracey Radford. (© Barney De La Cloche)